The Don't Freak Out Guide to Parenting Kids with Asperger's

By Sharon Fuentes

and

Neil McNerney, M.Ed., LPC

The Don't Freak Out Guide to

Parenting Kids with Asperger's

Copyright © 2013 by Sharon Fuentes & Neil McNerney

ISBN 978-0-9839900-4-8

Published by:

Integrated Publishing
38878 Mt. Gilead Rd., Leesburg, VA 20175
703-352-9002

Cover design by GKS Creative

Special Note:

Please remember that this book is not intended to give specific advice to your specific situation. It is a general guide intended to help families reduce stress related to having a family member with Asperger's. Please consult a professional counselor or family therapist for specific advice. All names and stories in this book, except for personal author stories, are composites and are not real people. Any similarities to actual people or incidents are purely coincidental.

From Sharon:

This book is dedicated to Jay, my Muse; to Grace, my Mini Me and to Roger, my Morty to his Lee!

From Neil:

This book is dedicated to all of those kids I have worked with over the years who are on the spectrum. Your ability to face your challenges and overcome obstacles is nothing less than heroic.

For more information about the authors, visit their websites:

www.aspieparenting.com

www.blog.mamasturnnow.com

www.reducehomeworkstress.com

www.neilmcnerney.com

CONTENTS

Introduction..1

Chapter 1: Don't Freak Out!..9

Chapter 2: Decoding Our Kids..27

Chapter 3: What Kind of Parent Are You?................................43

Chapter 4: The Pressures of Parenting an Aspie......................53

Chapter 5: Parenting an Aspie and Marriage...........................69

Chapter 6: The S.C.A.P.E Method.......................................77

Chapter 7: Early Interventions and Treatments........................85

Chapter 8: The School Years...101

Chapter 9: Siblings...123

Chapter 10: Valuable Insights from Adult Aspies....................135

Final Thoughts..155

Acknowledgements..157

Resources..... 161

INTRODUCTION

I would like to risk an assumption about why you are reading this book. You love your kids. Regardless of how prepared you thought you were for having children, the amount of love you feel for them still surprises you. Because of that love, you want to do everything you can to help your children succeed, grow and become productive members of society…you want them to be happy! But even though you love your kids, something is not working. This whole parenting thing is not going the way you thought it would. There is this child living with you that you know has your DNA yet may seem like a stranger to you. You're tired, feeling lost and perhaps even angry, and this overwhelmed sensation causes you to feel guilty. So when you saw the title of this book, you said to yourself, "If I can help my kid and learn how to not freak out, I'd like to know how to do it."

It was easy for me to make this assumption about you because I get it!

My son Jay's diagnosis was really no surprise to my husband and me. By the time we got the official paperwork, I already knew the answer. I had received my master's degree in "Google-ology" by then, taken every online test available and read whatever I could find. (For the record, there really is no such degree, but if there was, I could have received it.) All I needed was a real person with some fancy initials behind her name to make it official so that I could move on and get my boy the resources he needed.

I thought I was prepared that summer day when the psychologist called us into her office to go over the results of Jay's testing. But I soon learned that nothing really prepares you for the moment when you hear that your child has autism.

It's amazing how such a small word can have such a dramatic impact on our lives, and including vocabulary like high-functioning or Asperger's Syndrome doesn't help. Perhaps you are feeling this right now. Maybe you worry about whether or not you have what it takes to be the kind of parent that your child needs. Even worse, you may not have any idea what kind of parent that is! Confusion, anger, anxiety, even grief – you may be feeling them all!

I have been there. I understand. You see, it is part of the initiation we parents go through to join the club.

I wish I could tell you that the road ahead is going to be a smooth one, but I cannot. I wish I could promise you that it gets easier, but I cannot. What I can tell you is that you will find paths that have already been paved and learn to avoid the potholes in the ones that are not. I can tell you that you will discover that you are so much stronger than you ever imaged. I can tell you that, one day, you will realize that you really had nothing to "freak out" about. Most importantly: You are not alone!

What Will You Find in This Book?

An easier question to answer would probably be what won't you find in this book? What you won't find are terms you need to look up in a dictionary to understand. You won't find general assumptions. I don't know what my son, your daughter or any other person with Asperger's is feeling, what they need or what will always work for them, so I will never assume that I do. One thing this journey has taught me is that if you have seen one person with Asperger's, then you have seen one person with Asperger's. No two people are alike!

What you will find here is a book filled with real-life experiences. You will find tried and tested parenting advice on how to break the cycle of worry, anger and guilt. You will find a refreshing new way to view your child – as a person first. You will find effective techniques and tools on how to become a leader in your child's life. You will find hope, you will find support and, most importantly, you will find that you are not alone!

That summer day, as we got up to leave the psychologist's office, she stopped me and whispered into my ear, "Remember: he is still the same kid he was an hour ago." Then she handed me a copy of an essay written by Emily Perl Kingsley titled "Welcome to Holland." If you have not read this piece, I highly suggest you do. Do a simple online search, and it will pop up all over the place because it has become a mantra for many who are parents of special needs children. The story is simple but so meaningful. In it, you are asked to imagine you are getting ready for a trip.

For the sake of this book, let's say you are planning on going to China. You have wanted to go all your life. You have learned all about the Great Wall and the Forbidden City. You have even learned Mandarin in order to prepare you for your visit. Your bags are packed, and you excitedly board the plane.

It is a smooth flight with not even a bump from turbulence. That is why you are so shocked when upon arrival you hear the flight attendant say, "Welcome to Holland!" You are confused, perhaps even angry. How did you get here? What happened? This is not the way things were supposed to be. You had plans.

You imagined something completely different. You imagined China, not Holland.

When you get off the plane, it gets worse. You have to figure out how to communicate because you don't speak the language of this country. You feel angry, anxious and alone. At times you want to flee this strange land, but there are no return flights.

Days turn into months and months into years. Eventually, you learn to speak Dutch and find other people like you who thought they were going to China but also ended up in Holland. One day, you wake up, and it finally hits you: Holland is not a bad place; it is just a different place. Holland has windmills and beautiful tulips and so many other things that you never would have experienced in China. Holland is not a bad place; it is just different.

From time to time, you may hear one of your friends brag about her trip to China and how wonderful it was, and perhaps for a brief second, you feel a sense of longing for what might have been. But it fades quickly because you know deep in your heart how special Holland is, and you would not trade that for anything!

Welcome to the club, my friend! Welcome to Holland!

Before We Get Started – About the Authors

Wait, you might be saying, there are two authors listed on the cover of this book, but the introduction seems to have been written by just one person. You are very perceptive, my friend. When I approached Neil about working together to create a book that was in the same format as his wonderful book: *Homework - A Parent's Guide to Helping Out without Freaking Out,* the two of us racked our brains over how we would do this. How do we not confuse you, the reader? Since this is a parenting guide, we decided to write the book from the perspective of me, Sharon, the mother of a kid with Asperger's. The stories you will find are mine, but the tried and tested techniques come from Neil, the expert himself. Of course, I have tried them all, thus the tried and tested part. Is it starting to make some sense?

The book is written conversationally and hopefully will read exactly the way I talk. It should make you feel as if I am talking to you, my friend, because, well... I am! Although it was intended to be read from start to finish, I know the reality of our lives and that we may only have five minutes before the kids bust down the bathroom door. (You know you hide in there.) For that reason, we broke up the book into chapters and offer quick "Don't Freak Out" summaries at the end of each chapter. This will allow you to skip around or return to a certain section to re-read when you have more time. We also include resources, suggestions and additional exercises with many of the chapters.

Throughout the book you will see that I refer to my son either as having Asperger's/Autism or as an Aspie. There is much debate in the autism community over how the term autism is to be used when referring to individuals. Many choose to use the "person first" term by saying, "he is a person with autism" while many autistic adults note that autism is not a disease and not something that is separate from who they are, and feel that the terminology is not correct. Throughout this book you will see that I use both. It is in no way meant to be disrespectful to the autistic community; it is just that in our home the terms are interchangeable. My son will be the first to say that he uses AUTISM or ASPERGER'S as an adjective more than a noun. Jay has Asperger's in the same way he has brown hair and hazel eyes. It is part of who he is, but to him – and us – it does not define him. The term ASPIE, however, Jay does use as it gives him a group to which he feels he belongs.

Lastly, before we get started, I thought you might want to know who Neil and I actually are. When I read a book, especially a parenting book, I want to know a bit about the author. I ask myself, "Is this person credible? Do they have the credentials and experience to back up what they are saying?" So, let me tell you a bit about my dear friend Neil and myself.

About Neil McNerney, LPC

Neil is a licensed professional counselor who has been licensed in the state of Virginia since 1994. He spent seven years as a school counselor, dealing with most of the issues in this book. Neil is a member of the teaching faculty of the Virginia Tech Graduate School of Marriage and Family Therapy, where he teaches clinical techniques for working with children in a family context. He speaks and trains nationally and regularly provides workshops and keynotes at state and national professional conferences. He has helped to develop a parent-training program that is being used by hundreds of professionals worldwide. The main focus of Neil's work is increasing motivation in children and increasing the leadership skills of parents.

About Sharon Fuentes

 I am an award-winning freelance writer, special needs parenting expert and humor columnist for Westchester Family magazine (NY). My feature articles (which cover topics such as Dysgraphia, Autism Service Dogs, Vacationing with Special Needs Children, Dining Out with Allergies, Play-Based Learning, Using Visual Strategies, Social Stories and many more) have been published in regional, national and international publications. My personal essays on Asperger's have appeared in *Chicken Soup for the Soul - Raising Kids on the Spectrum* and Parenting magazine's special April 2013 1 in 50 edition. When I am not writing, you can find me speaking in public about autism acceptance.

What really qualifies me to write this book, even more than my years of professional experience, is the fact that I am a mom. I have two children: Jay, who is 12 and as you probably have already figured out has Asperger's, and Grace, who is 10 and oh my goodness doesn't! My life is rich with laughter, filled to the brim with love and has a good dose of autism thrown in there just to keep things interesting!

Chapter 1

Don't Freak Out!

Sharon and Jay's Story

"Did you know that if you weighed every living thing in the world, one-quarter of the mass would be ants?" my son Jay tells me, looking up over his phone and the Ripley's Believe It or Not app we finally allowed him to download. On and on he goes, rattling off interesting and odd facts. It is his new obsession, the thing he is most passionate about ever since we took him to Ripley's. He had seen the pamphlet at a rest stop on the highway and begged us for three days to take him there. Finally, we caved and, well, the rest is history.

The moment we stepped across the threshold and were met by an almost life-like replica of Robert Wadlow, the world's tallest man who reached 8 feet 11.1 inches in height, my boy was hooked. This friendly giant was followed by a full-size operational erector set Ferris wheel and a collection of shrunken human heads. Jay vowed to make it his mission in life to visit as many of the 90 different Ripley's across the US and 10 other countries as he could. Most parents, when they hear their children make statements like this, laugh it off as a silly naive fantasy. I know better!

Every Ripley's attraction or book starts off the same: "Some things will leave you speechless and wondering if what you just saw or read about could actually be true. There may not be words to describe it and even photos or video may still leave you saying 'Unbelievable.'" I honestly believe that every time a child is diagnosed with autism, the doctor should give the parents that same disclaimer. "Mr. and Mrs. So and So, your son has Autism…Believe It or Not?"

I must admit that at first we did not believe it.

Baby Gym Dropout

Jay was always considered special…from conception! It took me a while to get pregnant, and when I finally did, it was with twins. At 12 weeks I miscarried what would have been Jay's baby brother. The months of bed rest that followed were well worth it when at 34 ½ weeks my chubby little cherub made his enthusiastic entrance into the world, weighing in at a healthy 7lbs 11oz.

Jay was a sweet baby but, at the same time, very difficult. He was fussy and had terrible reflux. I may have been a nervous new mommy, but I knew that his giggles were real and not just gas! He was alert…so very alert. He was our perfect, long-awaited and much-loved angel. I eagerly quit my job so that I could stay home to be with him 24/7.

Eventually the 24/7 part proved to be a bit much, and this mama bear grew a bit stir crazy in her den. I needed to get out of the house, meet other new mommies and perhaps even take part in some conversations that did not include chapped nipples and diaper rash. So I signed us up for a baby gym class. I say "US" because I know now that this class was more for "ME" than Jay.

It was one of those places filled with disinfected-smelling in-door play sets, primary-colored ball pits, tunnels to climb through and a creepy-looking clown mascot that scared the bee-jeebies out of me. The teachers had soothing sing-song voices and smiled as they instructed us to play peek-a-boo or massage our babies using scarfs or whatever other product they wanted us to purchase at 20% off that week. My favorite part of these classes was circle time because we finally got to sit down, and the mamas were able to talk. Of course, the conversations always were about cracked nipples and diaper rash, but at that point I was willing to take what I could get.

Now, I am not knocking these types of classes. They can be an excellent outlet, especially for first-time mommies. Many of the moms I met there are still my friends today! But the problem with these places is that they tend to forget that not all babies reach milestones at the same time. Nothing gives a new mama more worries or feelings of inadequateness than realizing her baby is the only kid in the class that is not sitting up. The fact that my 6 month old was already saying words – "ball", "mama", even "banana" – was overlooked simply because he could not lift himself up.

The leader, whom I am almost positive had no real formal medical training, had a way of making me feel as if every instinct I had was wrong. She would smile and, with a hint of pity in her voice, say something like, "Well, some kids are late bloomers. He'll catch up, probably!" I would believe her and ignore the unreached milestone, and then the next one and the one after that. It is amazing who and what you choose to believe when you are not ready to see the truth!

A year passed, and we celebrated Jay's 1st birthday in grand style with an Old McDonald Farm theme which included a real petting zoo. Jay, of course, cried the entire time and refused to have anything to do with the animals. I made excuses that he was teething or that he had missed his morning nap. The other mommies bought it. Hey, I would have bought it except that I couldn't ignore that nagging feeling that perhaps it was more than that.

I remember watching the other babies crawling, some even toddling, all around the party, interacting with each other and the animals. Then there was Jay, dressed adorably in his blue jean overalls, sitting under a picnic table and playing contently with his blocks by himself. When I tried to coax him to play with the others, he would tell me, "No! Stay here!" So stay there he did.

It was easy back then to believe that nothing was different. He was just Jay, my beautiful brilliant baby. Even the pediatrician told me so.

"Sharon, your son is talking. Who cares that he's not crawling. He is so smart that he is going to skip that stage and get right to walking. Calm down and stop worrying."

"But, doctor, I read an article about the importance of babies crawling for at least 6 months before they start walking. Apparently there is some research that suggests that babies who don't spend enough time crawling are more likely to have ADHD and trouble with hand/eye coordination and even reading and writing," I whined back.

The doctor gave me the exact answer that I was looking for at the time, "You shouldn't read so much!" and dismissed my motherly instincts. I believed him because I was not ready to NOT believe him.

Finally, it was graduation day at baby gym. Our babies were going to be moving up to the toddler class where they would concentrate on new skills and social interactions. All the mommies had planned on going out to lunch together after class to celebrate.

I never made it to that lunch. During class the teacher pulled me aside and said that, although Jay was very smart, she did not think he was ready to move up to the toddler class. She pointed to the other babies who were running around the gym, climbing independently on the equipment and sliding down the baby slides. Then she pointed to Jay who was happily sitting in the ball pit, having what seemed like a very interesting conversation with himself. I could not help but smile as he seemed just so blissful. The teacher pulled me closer and whispered in my ear, "I am not supposed to say this, but I really like you and Jay, so, well, I am just going to come out and say it. Have you thought about having him tested? He just seems so different."

The way she said "different" made it sound like a bad word. As if he could sense me staring at him, Jay looked up, waved at me and said, "Hi, Mama!" Sure, he was different than the others. My boy was bright, charming and uniquely his own! I smiled politely at the instructor and respectfully said, "No need to worry about us moving up to the other class. We will not be coming back. Any place that cannot appreciate "different" is not a place I want to be." I picked up Jay, and the two of us walked out of the gym without even looking back. Did I believe then that my boy had autism? No, not yet. But I did believe in my boy!

"SEAMS" Perfect

Jay did learn to walk and later learned to crawl. By the time he was two, he was a force to be reckoned with. Curious, head strong, funny and sweet were all words we used to describe him.

But he was also becoming meticulous about the way certain things had to be. His food could not touch, he refused to walk barefoot on the itchy grass, and I cannot begin to tell you how many hours we spent making sure that the seams on his socks were perfectly lined up on his toes.

The WHY stage was among us, and nothing evoked more questions than my ever-expanding belly. Jay wanted to know why we had to have a girl because he wanted a brother.

"SpongeBob is a boy, Mommy."

"Yes, Jay, SpongeBob is a boy."

"If you have a girl, she won't like SpongeBob 'cause she is not a boy!"

"Sandy is a girl, Jay. Sandy likes SpongeBob!"

No amount of arguing could convince Jay of this. He was very black-and-white in his thinking. There was no grey. We never really thought much about this as it was just his personality. He could repeat an entire episode of SpongeBob, word for word. He had to line up his stuffed animals in a certain order before he went to bed. He needed to have the seams of his socks lined up perfectly. We called those things "Jayisms."

Jayisms

Jay may not have wanted a little sister, but once she arrived, he could not help but fall in love with her. Gracie was a happy baby, and no one could make her smile more than her big brother. Jay doted on her. When I would sit down to nurse her, he would pull up his little rocking chair next to mine and pretend to nurse his stuffed animal. It was the most precious sight ever. The way the two of them interacted was amazing. Perhaps that is why I was so taken back when Jay's preschool teacher suggested to me that he be tested for autism.

I was angry. Not my boy. My boy made eye contact. My boy interacted with us. Sure, he would flap his hands when he was very excited about something. Yes, the sound of a fire truck could send him squealing under a table, seeking safety and comfort. So what if there were only about five foods that he would eat. These were Jayisms, not autism!

We took him to be evaluated because I wanted so desperately to go back to that preschool teacher to tell her she was wrong.

Jay was first diagnosed with Sensory Integration Disorder. The term Asperger's was thrown around at that time, but it did not stick. Well, it stuck in my head, but not as a label. We began early intervention: occupational therapy, physical therapy and speech three times a week. To Jay, it was play time. For me, it was hell. I honestly could not understand how it was helping. Or maybe I was still in denial and did not believe there was a problem to begin with? Ding, ding, ding…we have a winning answer, folks.

As Gracie got older, I could not help but see more and more differences in Jay. Grace met all of her "normal" milestones. She sat when she was supposed to sit, she crawled and she walked. I was not one to compare my children, but somehow I could not help doing it.

It was time to face the facts. My boy would be starting kindergarten in a public school soon, and I needed to have more answers. I began to search online, read everything I could get my hands on and talk to whoever would listen. The more I learned about Asperger's, the more confident I grew that Jay had it. You see, at that time I still believed that autism/Asperger's was something you got. It took some time for me to come to the realization that it is just part of who he is.

Square Peg, Round Hole

Even though there was not a shadow of doubt that my boy was an Aspie, we never pushed to get a formal diagnosis. He already had an IEP in place, so I figured, why bother? As long as he was getting the help, the modifications and the tools he needed to succeed, I didn't care about the diagnosis. Then Jay entered 3rd grade, and well, that way of thinking changed.

That year the other children started to notice Jay's quirky behaviors and uncontrollable emotional outbursts. But even more importantly, Jay was starting to notice. He was not sleeping at night, his anxiety level was at an all-time high and his self-confidence was dangerously low. One day, in the middle of a meltdown, my boy blurted out, "I feel like I am a square peg trying to fit into a round hole, and no matter how hard I try to make myself fit, I can't do it. Why am I like this, Mommy?" My heart broke for my son. Not believing was no longer an option. We took him to be officially diagnosed.

Our journey thus far has been one filled with head-scratching, mind-boggling, unexplainable curiosities and events, much like the exhibits in one of Ripley's Odditoriums. Every day we are redefining normal. What is normal for our family may seem odd to the outside world, and that is okay! Finally, I can understand why my son can relate to Robert Ripley, his attractions and books. Ripley embraced the unknown, celebrated the unpredictable, pushed boundaries and forced people to see things in a different way. Square pegs in round holes are applauded in Ripley's world.

"Mom, did you know that North Korea and Cuba are the only countries on earth where Coca-Cola is not sold? Did you know that the venom of the Australian Cone Snail can cause instant paralysis and potential death and that there is no known antidote? Did you know…?" On and on my boy goes, stating fact after unbelievable fact, pushing boundaries, forcing people to see things in a different way. My boy is indeed, unbelievable!

If you only get one thing from my story, and from this book, I hope it is the strength to believe! Believe in yourself, believe in your instincts and, above all, believe in your child! Oh and another thing: Don't Freak Out!

Why Staying Calm Does Wonders

Experts say that the best way to help our children is simply to not freak out. Okay, maybe the experts didn't use that term, but that was what they meant. What they do say is that we need to be under control. Notice I did not say "in control," but rather "under control."

I never really thought there was a difference until Neil pointed it out. Under control means that **you** are in control **of yourself** instead of someone else being in control. This is a concept that I know I am trying to teach my Aspie, but I never really gave much thought as to how it applied to me. When you think about it, it is huge!

When you are under control, you are sending the message that regardless of what is happening, whether it is a meltdown in the middle of the grocery store or a fight over homework, you are deciding how you feel about it and how you will react. When we stay calm and under control, we keep the focus on our children.

I want to share with you a letter that I wrote several years ago when I was just starting my Autism journey. I share it with you so that you see that I really do understand what it is like. I understand how hard it is to stay calm and under control when you are tired, stressed and see your child hurting.

Dear Autism,

Hey there, "A," how are you doing? Listen, I don't mean to be rude, but do you think that perhaps for just a few days you could take a hike, get lost or go on a vacation?

Most days, Autism, I don't mind you being around. You are a part of my boy. I love him just the way he is, so that means you too. But the thing is…I am at my wit's end, Autism. Seriously, I am done.

I am exhausted and just don't have the oomph to deal with all the baggage you bring. Let's face it, you do bring a lot of crap with you. The meltdowns, the anxiety, the anger. You filled your suitcases to the brim with them, Autism. Some days your stuff is flung around our house so much that there is nowhere to walk, nowhere to hide. These are the days that I don't feel like being such a gracious hostess. I want you to pack your stuff and get out. And don't let the door hit you on the way out.

So here is the thing, Autism. I am asking, no begging, you to go stay somewhere else. I don't really care where you go. Please, Autism, just give him a few days of rest. A few days where my boy can fall asleep at night and stay asleep. A few days without feeling anxious and angry. Just a few days so that we all can catch our breath and remember what it feels like to do things without your heavy backpacks filled with all your stuff weighing us down. I'll even pay for your plane ticket.

Warmest regards,

MAMA

For the most part, I am able to stay under control by writing, but there are days, many days, when no amount of writing will help. These are the days when I am unable to take my emotions out of the equation. My voice rises, and my temper flares. I never feel good after losing my temper with my children. In fact, I feel the exact opposite, guilt, remorse, regret and many other negative feelings. I also know that my boy does not react well when I yell. It sets him off even further, which only increases my guilt, my remorse, my regret, etc.

There has been some very compelling research as to what happens to us when we lose our tempers. It used to be thought that losing one's temper was a type of release. We used to think that releasing all that bottled up emotion was a good thing and far better than holding it all in. But recent research is actually telling us the opposite.

There are two major types of mood chemicals in our brains: endorphins and cortisols. Endorphins are the good mood chemicals. They help us to relax, to stay focused, decrease pain and lots of other good stuff. Cortisols tend to do the reverse. They are released during stressful times and increase blood pressure, decrease mood, increase inflammation and other bad things.

When we lose our tempers, the amount of endorphins being released in our brains decreases, and the amount of cortisols released increases. This lasts up to 4 hours after someone loses his temper. So for 4 hours after I lose my temper or my son loses his temper, it is likely that both of us will actually feel worse because we just shot our brains with big doses of bad mood.

Kind of makes a lot more sense now, right? When we stay calm, we keep the focus on our children, not ourselves. We can, therefore, help our children to calm down themselves.

Exercise time. No I am not going to ask you to drop and give me 50, but if you want to do that, go right ahead. This is a mental exercise. I want you to think about the last three times you lost your temper with your child. Go ahead and write down what you did or said each of those times.

1._____

_____

_____

2._____

_____

_____

3._____

_____

_____

Now, think about how your child reacted or what might have been going on in your child's head after each outburst. I asked my Jay how he felt after a recent episode that ensued when he insisted he needed a new book for a school project even though he had 5 million perfectly good books already available. His response was that he was confused and instead of thinking about the real issue at hand and what I was trying to say to him, all he was thinking about was why I was so angry and how he had disappointed me. Disappointing me made him feel worse and therefore escalated his meltdown. I had a perfectly good opportunity to be a leader, a living, breathing, social story if you will. But instead, my temper made the situation about me, not him.

A true leader is a motivator. Actually, a true leader is someone who can inspire and foster self-motivation. Sure, I convinced my son to agree to use one of the books he already had, but he agreed to it because he thought he was disappointing me if he did not. He was other-motivated, not self-motivated. An other-motivated child needs to be pushed to do his homework, brush his teeth and take a shower. A self-motivated child learns how to do things without having to rely on someone else's actions to jump start it. Isn't that what we are all shooting for really –raising children who are able to function in this world independently? We are much more able to instill self-motivation by being calm as opposed to being reactive.

How Do You Stay Calm?

Saying you should remain calm is one thing; doing it is an entirely different one. It is much easier said than done. In order to stay calm, we need to first figure out what is causing us to get upset in the first place.

When you stop and think about it, most of our outbursts are rooted in our worry.

Worry is a good emotion at times, especially when it motivates us to do something different about our actions. For example, if I worry that something I have written is not good enough, it will motivate me to edit my work and perhaps allow me to catch a misspelled word and misplaced comma. If I worry because I have not heard from my parents in Florida in a long time, it will motivate me to make a phone call or perhaps plan a visit to see them. So, worries can be good, but only when we focus on ourselves and the worry leads us to change OUR OWN actions.

The problem is that most of our worry, when it comes to our children, is not based on our actions. Our worries are based on the actions of our children or (in a lot of cases) their lack of actions. We worry about how they will react in a certain situation, what they will do if they are confronted by bullies and what their future holds. We worry over the big issues, like whether or not they will graduate from high school, go to college and live on their own. These worries seep out of us over minor things like an unmade bed or a wet towel on the floor.

Suggestion: Put a Fence Around your Worries

Just like dogs need fences in order to stay where we want them to stay, our worries need fences, too. If we don't put a fence around our worries, then we can lose control of them, and who knows what type of havoc that might cause.

Here is an example of a time that I did not build a fence around my worry and the result of that negligence. Every August, I always get anxious. The idea of having to go through "teaching" a new set of teachers about my boy and sometimes about Asperger's is overwhelming. The year before Jay started 4th grade was unusually stressful for me. The "what-ifs" and "am I doing the right things" would keep me up all night. I was running on two, maybe three hours of sleep a day, which certainly did not help my mental state. The ironic thing was that I thought I was doing a really good job keeping my worry to myself. I soon realized that this was most definitely not the case.

Two weeks before school started, my son started having nightmares. Shortly after that, my daughter started having nightmares, too. Basically, no one was sleeping in our house.

We were snapping at each other, yelling, and let's just say it was not a happy home. Finally, one day I broke down. We were at Target, buying back-to-school supplies, and my kids were arguing over folders and notebooks when I snapped. I left the basket with all the supplies, grabbed their hands and practically dragged them to the car. When I got in, I happened to look in my rear view mirror and saw both my children silently crying, too scared to even sniffle aloud. I started to cry myself. I unbuckled, got out of the car and hopped into the back seat with my kids. I held them to my chest and told them both how sorry I was for yelling at them.

My son looked at me and said, "What is wrong with me, Mama, that you are so afraid that I won't do well in school this year?" My anxiety, my fears about how the teachers would treat him, about whether he would make friends, about everything, was completely visible to him. He interpreted my fear as him being bad, not good enough and wrong. This was certainly not the message I wanted to be sending to him.

Every August I still get those anxious feelings in my stomach. But now, I put a fence around those worries. My belief in my children, in what they are doing, helps to keep the worry under control. I do what I can to make sure they are prepared, and then I let go. I cannot control what is going to happen in the future. I can only control how I choose to react to what is happening now.

Suggestion: Pause Between Action & Reaction

Step 1: What are your pre-temper indicators?

I want you to think for a moment about what might be the first indications that you are about to blow. Is it a thought, an emotion, a physical sensation? For me, I purse my lips tight, cross my arms and my foot starts to tap. My inner dialogue might be something like, "I can't believe you just did that." My face usually feels hot, and my breathing becomes much more rapid. My palms also get sweaty.

What about you? Write down three things that happen, inside or out, when you begin to feel like you might lose your temper.

1._____

2._____

3._____

Neil always tells his clients to write these things down on a small card or piece of paper and to keep it with them for a week. Whenever you come across the card, review the three pre-temper indicators. The more you see them, the more aware of them you will become and the easier the next step will be.

Step 2: Pause.

When you notice that your pre-temper indicators are happening, stop whatever you are doing. Don't say anything. Don't do anything. Okay, if you are driving a car or crossing a busy intersection, keep driving or walking. But for everything else, just wait! Don't say anything to your child, your husband or even your dog if it is indeed the dog that is setting you off.

For example, if you are driving home from school and your son announces, "By the way, I need a poster board for a school project that is due tomorrow," keep driving. Don't respond by yelling, "You are telling me this now?" Just pause. Wait until you have grown completely calm before you respond. If you react immediately, you will set him off. If you are both upset, nothing will get accomplished, especially the school project.

Don't Freak Out

Chapter One Summary

- There is no denying it: We are better leaders when we are calm. It's our responsibility to keep ourselves calm, not the responsibility of our children.
- The two ways to keep your worries under control:
    - Put a fence around your worries, and
    - Pause between action and reaction.

Chapter 2

Decoding Our Kids

In this chapter we are going to start talking about our kids. While no two people with Asperger's are alike, there are some characteristics, or coping styles, that they share. I like the term "styles" because it suggests that they may change from time to time, day to day, and moment to moment. For each Aspie style, there is a parenting approach that tends to work best. The ability to recognize which style our Aspies are exhibiting at any given time makes it much easier to decide how to help and lead them. Knowing all of this will make more sense when we put it all together with the S.C.A.P.E method in Chapter 6, but for now, let's talk about the different styles of Aspies, the good parts (the Ups) and sometimes not-so-good traits (the Downs) that accompany them, and some parenting tips to try for each style. I'll even give you an example of how Jay has and still does fit into each of these styles.

Style #1: The Rule-Follower Aspie

While enjoying a wonderful summer day at a local water park, I made the mistake of taking out a bag of pretzels when my children mentioned they were hungry. Jay became frantic and started shoving the bag into my tote.

"What are you doing?" I asked him confused. "You just complained that you were hungry. You love pretzels. So what's the problem?"

Jay started to cry. I looked around our chairs and saw other families enjoying their snacks they had brought from home.

Even the Life Guard was enjoying a protein bar that he didn't buy from the snack bar. Surely this could not be because we brought these salty treats with us? I tried to reason with him.

"It's not like we brought a whole picnic. This is just a little snack to hold us over until we are ready to buy lunch from the Snack Bar." My boy grabbed my hand and had me follow him to the entrance, where the waterpark rules were clearly displayed. He pointed to number three: No outside food is allowed to be brought into the park. No amount of talking – and believe me I tried – was going to convince my boy that it was okay to eat those pretzels.

Jay, like many Aspies, is a rule follower, and I clearly had broken rule number three. We had an early lunch that day and saved the pretzels for the car ride home.

My son was not intentionally trying to be difficult. The Rule Follower simply must have rules to live by and will create his own if they are not provided. Rules are a way for the Rule Follower Aspie to manage his anxiety and uncertainty. They provide clear direction and understanding to a situation.

The Ups and Downs of the Rule Follower Aspie

The Rule Follower is usually a teacher's dream student. The rule follower respects authority figures and does well when it is perfectly clear who is in charge. Problems tend to arise for these kids, however, when they become the Rule Police and begin to tell on others. They feel the need to monitor and enforce the rules for everyone. Outbursts and meltdowns can occur when rules are vague or absent. Outbursts can also occur when the person in charge lacks authority in the Rule Follower's eyes.

One of the issues that kids with Asperger's have is a difficulty with nuanced situations. This causes problems because there are so many nuances in real life:

- If the speed limit is 25, why are we going 28?
- When the teacher tells us to be quiet, we should all be quiet.
- No sharing food at lunch means no one should share food.
- My sister should be punished every time for being sassy.

Life for a Rule Follower is extremely stressful and complicated. We tend to take nuances for granted, but for a Rule Follower, nuances are like living in a foreign country.

Parenting Tips for the Rule Follower Aspie

Rule followers crave structure and routine. Something as simple as listing on a chalk board you display in the kitchen what is for dinner each night of the week can really help the Rule Follower Aspie feel more centered. As I said before, meltdowns are a result of changes to routine, and flexibility is usually something that does not come easily to this Aspie. With this in mind, make sure your child understands that this is a tentative menu and that some days you may need to flip-flop entrees or even order out for pizza. Simply erasing and rewriting the correct option on the board is most likely all it will take to get this Rule Follower back on track. We use this menu calendar with Jay in our home, and I no longer have to hear "what's for dinner?" every morning when he wakes up. He simply goes to the board in the kitchen and looks for himself. He is then able to create a picture in his mind's eye as to how his day will proceed.

The most important thing you can do as a parent is to help your rule follower see that the world has many other colors, not everything is black and white. Using social stories and informing your children of what is expected to happen but reminding them that things could change is key. Fortunately, your rule follower already knows how to follow rules; you just need to concentrate on helping him become a more independent thinker with better problem-solving skills so he can make good choices on his own.

Style #2: The Anxious Aspie

Before Jay knew he had Asperger's, he was having a lot of difficulty falling asleep. We tried everything; nothing helped. You see, the more Jay couldn't sleep, the more anxious he became about it. He would stare at the clock, which of course made him so upset that slumber eluded him even more. The lack of sleep caused him to spiral even more out of control. It was a vicious cycle that none of us really understood and certainly none of us knew how to fix.

Amazingly, his sleep issues improved after we finally told him he had Asperger's. At first I did not understand this correlation. Now it makes complete sense to me. The Anxious Aspie usually becomes stressed when he is feeling a lack of something as in "lack of sleep," "lack of confidence," "lack of control," "lack of rules," "lack of understanding" and so on. Jay was experiencing so many of these. He knew something was different, and the other children in school were certainly not afraid to point those differences out to him. He was feeling all of the "lack ofs" at once. No wonder the poor child could not sleep at night, becoming emotional and prone to melt downs.

The Ups and Downs of the Anxious Aspie

Everyone, both neurotypical (a term used to describe us folks who do not have any so-called neurological deficiencies, thus making us "typical") and Aspie, experiences anxiety from time to time. As we mentioned in chapter one, anxiety can be a good

30

thing if it is used in the right way. The Anxious Aspie, who is afraid of getting bad grades, may choose to study more on her own, which is a very good thing. However, if that anxiety occupies so much of the child's thoughts that it causes her to become hyper-vigilant and unforgiving of any school slip-ups, well, you can see how quickly this can go downhill. Before you know it, you have a child who is experiencing a bunch of "lack ofs:" a lack of confidence because "I'm an idiot; I got a bad grade," a lack of understanding because "How can this be possible? I studied?" a lack of control because "What am I going to do now? What will happen to me? Will I get into a college, get a good job and have a good life?" The brain won't shut down or let this go until all those "lack ofs" are taken care of.

When the brain is on overdrive, there is bound to be a night of no sleep. A night of no sleep means that there will most likely be more meltdowns and emotional outbursts the next morning. All of these factors will take a toll on the student's school work, which will make the Anxious Aspie even more anxious, and, well, you can see where this is going.

Parenting Tips for the Anxious Aspie

The first tip I have for you is to never, ever tell the Anxious Aspie to "calm down." Although well meaning, this tends to be as effective as telling a hungry baby to stop crying. Instead, talk softly and slowly as your Aspie's brain is most likely already on overload and you don't want to overwhelm him anymore. Together, try to figure out the "lack ofs." What is it that your Aspie is not getting that he needs? Does he not understand a social situation? Are there no rules in place? Did he not get enough sleep the night before?

Once you understand what is lacking, you can then try to gently lead your child in the right direction. I say gently because, if you are too abrupt or certain about your opinions, your Aspie is sure to dismiss them quickly. Example: If you tell your Aspie he is overly tired and should lie down, you are certain to be met with resistance. Instead gently lead him. "I have an idea. How about we read a few pages of your book together? We can do it lying on your bed where it is more comfortable."

With all the "lack ofs" checked off, your child is bound to feel less anxious. Take the example I mentioned about Jay and his not sleeping. Once Jay had a diagnosis, a name as to what this difference he was feeling was, he now had an understanding. (That's one "lack of" checked off.) With this diagnosis and new understanding, he gained a sense of confidence as he belonged to a group for the first time (another check).The more we all learned about Asperger's and about Jay, the more we realized that he craved structure, routine and rules, and we were quick to provide him with these things whenever possible (check).

We also found a few calming techniques that work well with him: guided imagery and the use of a weighted blanket*. A simple mind trip to the beach led by me and his ten pound weighted blanket was all it took to lull my boy to sleep (check and check). No longer "lacking" anything, Jay was able to sleep better and most nights still does.

---

*Guided Imagery is a process in which thoughts and suggestions are used to guide the person's imagination toward a relaxed, focused state. Since many Aspies tend to think in pictures, this is a highly-effective technique to be used to teach your child to self-calm. Weighted blankets are considered therapeutic and are made with weights to provide a proprioceptive (awareness of one's body position in space) input to the body. It is, Jay says, like getting a nice tight hug. To find out more on these techniques, check out the resource section of this book for websites and recommendations.

Style # 3: The Analytical Aspie

Remember the terrible two stages, during which a child is constantly asking, "Why?" Why is the sky blue? Why does water have no taste? Why is my hair brown? While most kids seem to outgrow this stage, the Analytical Aspie does not. In fact, his coping style is to try to make sense of the world around him by using logic, reasoning and rational thoughts. Rules alone are not enough; the Analytical Aspie must know the thinking process behind them. If you ask him to do something, he will want to know why. It is not that he is trying to be ornery; thoughtlessly accepting your rules is just not the way he functions. If your answer is too illogical, he most likely will not listen.

The Ups and Downs of the Analytical Aspie

This child is extremely bright, no question about it. He usually becomes agreeable once he understands the reasoning behind something. However, he may tend to be a bit stubborn because he usually has his own reasons and explanations for things. You will have to be very convincing to get him to change his mind once this happens.

The biggest downside to this style is that the Analytical Aspie tends to "overanalyze" everything. Because of this tendency, he can become stuck in an "analysis phase" and not progress to the actual "action phase." I have a great story to use as an example for this.

When Jay was in 5th grade, his class went on a team building fieldtrip. There were challenges set up that were intended to, well, challenge the kids. The activity that Jay and all the other students were most excited about trying was the zip-line where, once safely clipped into harnesses, they would walk across a high wire and then glide from platform to platform by way of a free-moving pulley suspended on cables high above the ground. Just writing that makes me queasy as I don't like heights; that was why I sent my hubby as the chaperon for that trip.

My husband came home and told me the story of how he noticed that Jay, who wanted to be first for every other activity, was constantly moving back, allowing other kids to cut in front of him in line. Not sure what the problem was, he approached Jay. Jay's mind was going a million miles an hour trying to process this unfamiliar situation. Jay was stuck in a "what and what if" stage. "What is the purpose behind this? What will I gain by doing this successfully? What will happen if I fall? What if my harness comes undone? What if the wind picks up? What if I decide to not do it?" His need to reason, to be logical, was causing him anxiety and keeping him from doing something he was so excited to try. My hubby simply told our boy, "Stop thinking and just do it!" And so, my boy just did it. To this day he still talks about the experience and how free he felt flying through the trees like a bird.

Parenting Tips for the Analytical Aspie

As you can see from the example I just used, many times your job will be to help your child see how unproductive overanalyzing can be. If he wants to soar like a bird, he is going to just have to do it. As your Analytical Aspie gets older, you are going to have to do much more research and explaining because rules alone will no longer mean as much. Helping your child see things from a new different angle is what you want to strive for. Once they have all the information, they can then make their own rational and, of course, very logical decisions themselves.

Style# 4: The Fictional World Aspie

This Aspie uses distractions to take him away from the real world. When things become too stressful or confusing in the here and now, he takes comfort in the familiarity of his fantasy world. Most of the time he does this by use of some type of electronic equipment: Xbox, iPad, computer. He can also lose himself in a good book or by listening to music. But this creative child does not need an actual object to experience this delicious escape. He has no problem replaying his favorite movie in his head and can even recite the script word-for-word. If you interrupt his fantasy world, you just may feel his wrath.

The Ups and Downs of the Fictional World Aspie

Here is where I may differ from other experts. You see, I have no real problem with the Fictional Aspie coping style. I admire the power of imagination and believe that many strokes of genius have occurred because of this. Think about the way that Albert Einstein lost himself in Math and Science, Mozart in music or Picasso in painting. We strive to help our children find ways to calm themselves, and for many of our kids, this is it. That said, there are a few downsides. If we constantly allow our kids to live in their own worlds, we risk them missing out on things that are happening in ours. It is a fine balance we need to obtain. Below is an example of how Jay, my boy who has a very vivid and active fictional world, used his fantasy friends to help him from melting down in public.

We live in Northern VA, which is a history buff's dream. While Jay loves to learn about the past, he prefers to live in the Sci-Fi future. Unfortunately for him, he is not the only member of our family, which means that he needs to compromise from time to time. This is not an easy thing for any child, least of all an Aspie.

We decided to take a trip to Williamsburg to celebrate Grace's birthday. We figured a visit to the amusement and water park there would be enticing enough to get both kids through the historical tours as well. For the most part it did, until it didn't. It was hot, really hot, and we had been walking around for a very long time. The newness of the period actors and reenactments had worn off, and Jay wanted to go back to the hotel and go swimming. But Grace was not done. She wanted to take one more guided tour through the gardens. My husband offered to take Jay back to the hotel so that Grace and I could leisurely enjoy our stroll through the roses, but this was a family vacation and I wanted the entire family to be a part of it. So, I paid the admissions, and we all went in.

I thought that once we were inside, the tranquility of the gardens would calm Jay and he would be okay. I thought he would want to try to pump the well and carry the water from the bucket the way the other kids were lining up to do. Jay was done with our world though. He had reached his limits, and his tolerance thermometer had reached boiling. Before he blew his lid, he did something that I admit, at first, I found a bit embarrassing. He sat down smack in the middle of the path and took out his book and began to read. He did not notice people having to walk around him or looking at him strangely as there was a bench just three feet from where he sat. Nope. He happily sat there on the ground, reading his book and flapping away in his excitement.

As I watched my boy, it finally hit me. I wanted so desperately to have a so-called "normal" vacation, but guess what? We aren't normal, and that is okay. My boy was engaged with us for the entire beginning part of the day. He must have worked very hard to do that as this strange place was as far from his every day routine as one could possibly get. Instead of feeling embarrassed, I suddenly felt so proud. My boy could have easily lost it. If you think about it, he had every reason to lose it. But instead, when he started feeling overwhelmed, when he had already expressed to me what he needed to feel better (going back to the hotel, which I had ignored), he did the next best thing – he took out his book. That was self-advocacy at its best. I did suggest that he move to the bench so that he would not get stepped on, which, after some consideration, he reasoned was a logical request and complied. With Jay happy, lost in his familiar fictional world, the rest of us were able to enjoy the garden tour.

Parenting Tips for the Fictional World Aspie

This Aspie's fictional world has many functions. In addition to being a source of entertainment and enjoyment, it also can be used has a calming technique. Before it is used as that, it is extremely important that you make sure your child understands the difference between make-believe and real life. Using the reward of reading his book for 10 minutes after he finishes his math homework and before he starts his English is perfectly fine. It lets his overworked brain relax a bit. But when the timer goes off and little Johnny is so lost in the pages of Harry Potter that he argues and fights when you ask him to close the book, it may be time to consider limiting his fictional world intervals. Our goal as parents is not to change our Aspies but to give them tools that will help them interact and be a part of the real world. Using fictional fantasy life as a coping style is fine as long as it doesn't interfere with that objective.

Style # 5: The Doom, Gloom and Boom Aspie

Everyone has bad days during which they feel blue or that life has let them down. Unfortunately, our Aspies tend to have a few more of these days than the average Joe. Since many of our kiddos just don't understand or know what to do with these negative feelings, they are prone to acting out. The Doom, Gloom and Boom Aspies tend to see the glass as half empty instead of half full. They may feel as if the whole world is out to get them; therefore, they are on a constant offense mode, ready to attack before anyone attacks them. They fight with others, verbally and often physically, as a way to gain a sense of control. Their emotions definitely determine their actions. Below is an example of how much our kids do feel and how it can affect their behavior.

Jay was in art class when he suddenly noticed that his special pencil was missing. Immediately, the fact that the pencil was missing meant to Jay that someone in his group had stolen it. They knew how much this pencil meant to him – remember, I'm speaking from Jay's point of view – and they took the pencil anyway. Jay became upset and angry and announced to the entire group, "I know one of you stole my pencil. You have until the end of the class to return it or else I will rip your heads off!" Then he sat down.

A student, understandably so, reported Jay's threat to the teacher, and Jay was sent to the Vice Principal's office. This is where you will get some insight into how the Doom, Gloom and Boom Aspie's brain works. Jay understood what he did was wrong. He admitted that it was a bad choice and even apologized. What he could not understand was how the other boy could have felt threatened. "Mom, there is no physical way I could ever really rip his head off. It was just words. Why would he get so upset?" My very literal boy.

I remember asking Jay what was so special about this pencil that would cause him to accuse others and risk getting into trouble for it. My son stopped and looked at me with a look that would melt your heart – in fact it did. "Mom, before we left Brazil, my friend Daniela gave me that pencil. She said to remember her when I use it. How can I remember her if the pencil is gone?" Once again, my literal boy.

The Ups and Downs of the Doom, Gloom and Boom Aspie

It might be hard to see many positives when you are dealing with a Doom, Gloom and Boom Aspie, however, many artists, musicians, actors and comedians have made their livelihood embracing their pessimistic emotional ways. Knowing that doesn't make the whininess, bossiness, tantrums and arguments you are dealing with today any better though, does it? Besides, who wants to be around a downer? The reality is that a child who is feeling like this is prone to even more depression as the demands of adulthood fall upon his already-burdened shoulders. Just because your child is going through this style now, doesn't mean he will tomorrow, especially if he has a parent like you employing the tips below.

Parenting Tips for the Doom, Gloom and Boom Aspie

The first thing you need to do is validate your Aspie's feelings. No matter how silly I may have thought it was, Jay had a very real emotional attachment to his pencil. No amount of persuasion on my part would convince him that losing it would not take away his memory of his friend. So, I validated his feelings first. "Jay, I can only imagine how sad you must feel because you lost that special pencil. I am so sorry for your loss." Jay instantly calmed down as now he felt understood and was ready to listen to what I had to say next.

After getting a Doom, Gloom and Boom Aspie's attention, you can calmly and very matter-of-factly address the particular issue at hand. Focus only on this issue; don't let the conversation get side-tracked. If you Aspie tries to argue during the conversation, remain calm and remember that this is coming from his sense of anxiety, not him purposely trying to be argumentative or rude. Most of the time it really is not what you are talking about that matters anyway, but rather what is going on behind the content that is important. For Jay it was about missing his friend, feeling lonely in his new school and sensing that he did not belong.

Accept your child for the wonderful person she is now. Make sure to point out the fabulous qualities that make her uniquely beautiful. Show her how the glass is half full, not half empty. All these things will help to build self-confidence. When you feel good about yourself, it is much easier to feel positive about others and the world in general.

Steve Jobs once said, "You can't connect the dots looking forward; you can only connect them looking backwards. So you have to trust that the dots will somehow connect in your future." Above all, our job is to teach our kids to trust that the dots will connect in the future. Those dots may not form a straight line when they do, but straight lines are boring anyway!

Don't Freak Out

Chapter Two Summary

- Our Aspies' styles will give us great insight about how they are feeling and what they need at any given moment.

- Those styles include The Rule Follower Aspie, The Anxious Aspie, The Analytical Aspie, The Fictional World Aspie and The Doom, Gloom and Boom Aspie.

- Our Aspies' styles will fluctuate. As they do, we need to adjust our approaches. As no child is expected to be perfect, no single parenting style will work universally.

- We just need to have patience and above all not freak out!

Chapter 3

What Kind of Parent Are You?

I want you to ask yourself, "What kind of parent am I?" to help you examine how you deal with your children during the tough times. When things are going well, when our kids are happy and not having problems in school, it is easy to say, "I am a great Mom. Heck, I would even go as far as to say that I am a mom of the year candidate." But what about during the tough times, when homework isn't getting done, when no one is sleeping at night and the backtalk is being served on a platter like a side of fries? These are the moments when our real parenting styles tend to come out. Here is a humorous column that I wrote for *Westchester Family* magazine a while ago.

Mommy Jail…when a time out isn't enough!

I recently had an "I'm ready for a glass of wine at 9am" kind of morning. It started with waking up to the whistle of the crossing guard outside my bedroom window. After finally coming out of my coma-like state, I realized my alarm never went off. I jumped out of bed and into the nearest set of clothes that were conveniently hanging from the treadmill. (See, it is good for something.) Another glance at the clock confirmed that I had only 20 minutes to get my kids up, dressed, fed and sitting with their hands crossed nicely in front of them at their desks at school.

I dashed downstairs and threw two Pop-Tarts in the toaster. I took out the milk for my daughter and juice for my lactose intolerant son. Shoot...milk had gone bad. I spent three minutes doing the nose-to-carton test, trying to determine just how bad it really was. I eventually caved and gave into the pressure of the suggested expiration date, and down the sink it went. Of course, there was not enough juice for them both, what with it being Murphy's Law and all. Water...she would have water.

With my makeshift breakfast now on the table, I turned my attention to lunchboxes. Thankfully, I had prepped them the night before and only had to warm up the leftover spaghetti. I stuck the container in the microwave and dashed upstairs to see how the troops were faring. Halfway through my cheerleading chant, which went something like, "Brush Your Teeth, Comb Your Hair, and Put Your Socks On," I heard a popping noise and smelled something burning. Shoot...the leftovers were in an aluminum container! When I opened the microwave door, the smoke from the smoldering aluminum caused the smoke detector go off, which made both kids frantic, and down the stairs they rushed, without brushing their teeth, combing their hair or putting their socks on. I took a few yoga breaths, pasted on a fake smile and encouraged the children to calm down and to please hurry up and eat. That is when my son suddenly felt the need to point out just how bad a job I was doing.

"Let's face it, Mom, you are not doing so great. The house smells, you're stressed and I had no fresh towels this morning!"

I snapped! For the first time in my life, I could truly understand why some animals eat their young. I love my children, but at that moment, all I wanted to do was lock myself in my bedroom and not come out until they were ready to go to college. I closed my eyes and tried to compose myself, and as I did, I had this vision of Mommy Jail!

Imagine your very own space, a freedom cell where you could actually finish a cup of coffee, a phone conversation, a thought, without being interrupted. You would receive three meals a day, which you would not have to cook or – even better – clean up! Sure, you would be locked up, but that would mean your kids would be locked out!

"Earth to Mom. We are going to be late for school," my son bellowed, forcing me back to reality. Faster than a speeding bullet, I threw a granola bar into each of their lunchboxes and shoved them out the door and into my car.

While sitting in the drop off lane, I couldn't help but smile as my thoughts went back to my fantasy of Mommy Jail. I even came up with a commercial jingle.

Mommy Jail, when the going gets tough and Mom has had enough! Don't delay, call today. Our operators are standing by!

My imaginary bubble burst when the car behind me honked for me to move forward. The kids unbuckled and were about to get out of the car when my daughter stopped. She gently planted a sticky strawberry Pop-Tart kiss on my cheek and said, "Hope you have a better day, Mommy." As I watch them walk into school, it dawned on me: I'm already doing time for my crime. And you know what? The inmates are pretty darn cute!

While a funny story that did lead to some great writing material, it was not my best parenting moment. Some days when I am overwhelmed, I overreact, yell, blame and sometimes wish I could be locked away. Knowing this is the first step towards changing my manner of parenting to a style that will be more beneficial to my children and to me.

Which brings us back to the question I asked earlier, "What kind of parent are you?" Below is a parenting style toolbox. As you read through these, you will probably see some of yourself in many, if not all, of them. That's okay. In fact, that is pretty normal and ideal. The goal of taking a look at this is to understand yourself a little better when it comes to the inevitable trials and tribulations that you will face with your Aspie and any other children too.

The Calm Parent

This is the one we all strive to be. The Calm Parent is the person who can deal with whatever comes her way with an unruffled demeanor. She doesn't take bad grades personally, she doesn't get anxious when she sees the school's number appear on her caller ID, and she doesn't get angry when her child has a meltdown in the middle of the supermarket, causing her to leave without her groceries. She realizes that her child's actions are not about her; they stem from her son being overstimulated, overly tired or frustrated. She is the parent we all make every effort to be, and on our best days, we are her as deep down we all know that staying calm truly is the best way to deal with our Aspies. I like to say that I am the Calm Parent...until I'm not!

The Anxious Parent

Almost all of our feelings that cause us distress when it comes to our kids are based on one emotion: WORRY! Worry, fear, anxiety, whatever you call it, is all the same. It's that lousy feeling we get when we think about our child's future. As the parents of special needs children, we tend to spend a lot of time being anxious. We worry about how we will pay for therapy, whether or not teachers are following the IEPs, what is happening on the bus rides to and from school, will our children finish high school, go to college, get married and live independently.

What will happen when we are no longer around to take care of them? It is no wonder we are so tired in the morning. Who can sleep with all that worry lying next to us?

The biggest problem with being anxious about our kids is that anxiety is extremely contagious. Our anxiety will quickly become our kids' anxiety. Even if our anxiety is reduced, our kids' anxieties will increase, sometimes to unhealthy levels.

The Angry Parent

Believe it or not, there is not much difference between the Angry Parent and the Anxious Parent. Both are worriers, but that worry manifests itself in different ways. Where the anxious parent hovers, the angry parent yells. For example, if I ask an Aspie of an angry parent why he wants to do well in school, he might reply, "Because I don't want my mom to yell at me!"

Yelling, "Why did you leave your wet towel on the floor again? Go pick it up now!" may make the immediate situation better as, most likely, the Aspie will go pick it up, but it is a temporary fix as the child is only behaving in an effort to calm the parent and make things more comfortable for himself (all that yelling is hurting his ears).

Sometimes this type of parenting style may actually have the opposite effect that we desire on our Aspies and make things worse. In many cases, a parent's freaking out will actually escalate an Aspie's frustration and incite even more of a meltdown. If you are the parent of a Doom, Gloom and Boom Aspie, an angry parenting style is sure to make things a heck of a lot messier!

The Supportive Parent

This parent's main role is to be a support for her child. This is the positive affirmations mama on steroids. She assumes only the best about their child and searches for opportune moments to praise him. She is quick to be sympathetic when her Aspie comes home with a bad grade and tries to avoid giving advice unless asked. This style is important to learn as many of our Aspies tend to have low self-esteem and need additional reminders and boosts of confidence, but it is even more important to understand when and when not to use it.

For example, the supportive parent style works great for the responsible Aspie. By being supportive, the responsible Aspie will hear, "You can do this! I believe in you!" This type of support is helpful for them. But if you have an Aspie who is caught lying and is being defiant, this type of parenting style alone would not be very beneficial. If your child was just busted for cheating on a test, saying, "Oh, Johnny, I know you really wanted to do well on that test. I know you will do better next time," may not be the best response. A kid caught cheating needs some additional leadership from you so that he won't cheat again. Being supportive alone, without utilizing any other style, would not be helpful in this case.

The Blaming Parent

This is an easy parenting style for many special needs parents to fall into. We blame vaccines, environmental factors or whatever else the big "IT" that supposedly causes autism is at the moment. The problem with blaming, however, is that it usually does nothing to make things better. Blame yourself, and you will just feel even guiltier. If you blame the school, they will get defensive or tell you that is just the way they do things. Blame society and, well, nothing will happen since society is not really able to respond.

A parent who blames others will quickly produce a child who blames others for her problems. Our kids pick up these things very quickly. When we spend a lot of time trying to find someone or thing to blame, we send the message to our kids that the first thing they should do is find someone at fault rather than trying to figure out a solution to a problem.

The Consultant

The Consultant is more active than the Supporter. A consultant parent is being the supporter style parent while also providing information and advice. The Consultant gives her child a chance to try to be successful on his own, but after observing the roadblocks, adds some helpful advice that MIGHT be accepted.

The goal of this type of parenting style is to give advice that will be heard. Many Aspies have a hard time being wrong or corrected. A successful Consultant knows when is the right time to offer advice and when is not. She knows that a good time to offer advice and help is AFTER her child has calmed down. The worst time to consult would be any time her Aspie is upset, anxious or angry.

The Perfectionist

The perfectionist likes to have things – yup, you guessed it – PERFECT! Many of our Aspie kids have this trait. My son Jay does. The thing I did not see at first was that his perfectionist tendencies are not necessarily due to his Autism. They are a result of seeing me, his mom, exhibit many perfectionist traits. Monkey see, monkey do. Well, most of the time.

Kids of perfectionists tend to react in two ways. The first way is for the child to become a perfectionist himself (like my boy). The second way is to stop trying when they come to the conclusion that they can't measure up, even when trying their hardest. (My daughter was going this route.)

If you do have the perfectionist streak, like me, your best bet is to focus it inward instead of outward. How can I be the best parent I can be? Notice that I did not say PERFECT parent because, guess what? There is no such thing as a perfect parent. It's a myth passed down from generation to generation, like Big Foot or Bloody Mary!

The Boss

No, not Bruce Springsteen. The Boss Parent is still trying to be supportive and a consultant while maintain the upper hand and being able to dish out consequences. The Boss is able to calmly (there is that word again...calm) assess the situation and determine what is the appropriate reward or punishment.

Unfortunately, we tend to jump to the BOSS role way too quickly. It is a powerful tool if used correctly. In order to be the most effective and impart the most beneficial long-term effects, other parenting styles need to be put into practice before assuming the role of BOSS.

So, there you have it: the real life parenting roles we tend to fall into. Did you recognize yourself in any of these? In order to be effective parents, we need to understand that timing is everything. Timing is dictated by how our kids are managing a situation. What role we take on depends on the situation and how our children are managing that situation. We will explain this more when we put it all together in Chapter Six.

Don't Freak Out

Chapter Three Summary

- You have control over how you parent your child, especially through a challenging situation.
- The first step is to identify the type of parent you are.
- Next, you need to decide what adjustments you can make to be more effective.
- Assess each situation individually and choose which style of parenting best suits that particular situation.

Don't Freak Out Exercise

Neil has a great quiz on his website that helps you determine if you are being too soft, too firm or just right in your parenting. Check it out by going to:

www.reducehomeworkstress.com/exercises/just-right.

Chapter 4

The Pressures of Parenting an Aspie

I am not a morning person. My kids and hubby know this about me too. There is a reason why I wear a Grumpy nightshirt that says, "Don't talk to me until I have had my first cup of coffee!" And, if any extra morning drama occurs, well, let's just say this Mama Bear growls. I am not proud when I turn on my cubs. Unlike those stupid TV sitcoms where the house is always clean, the kids never have snotty noses and the mom's clothes are never stained with cheese puff fingerprints, I know that there is no studio track laughter in real life. No, I get tears, real tears that fall down their sweet cheeks and shoot daggers through my heart when I lose it. I wipe them away and do my best to fix whatever havoc I have somehow allowed to happen and then send them off to school. It is then, alone with my coffee, that I feel the most real…and guilty – I usually feel lots and lots of guilt!

Having kids was one thing. Raising them well is something entirely different. Parenting is hard work. Parenting a special needs child is even harder. Like any job, the quality of our performance reflects how much we put into it, how quickly we learn and how willing we are to adapt. But real life is not like those TV sitcoms. When we watch our shows, we do so knowing that everything will work out okay in the end. There are no guarantees of that happening in real life. That knowledge alone is enough to make you not want to get out of bed in the morning or, if you do get up, drink that second cup of coffee!

Everything today is more accelerated; more information-driven than experience-gathered as it was when we were growing up. Our parents did not have to worry about cyber predators or cyber bullying with us the way we do with our children. We have all the same pressures of parenting as our elders had: parental expectation, violence, substance abuse, but doubled. Add on the challenges related to having a child on the Autism spectrum, and it is no wonder we feel stressed.

This chapter and the one following it will touch on some of the more common pressures that parents of a child with Asperger's tend to face and how we can best overcome them.

Pressure # 1: The Diagnosis

The diagnosis usually is the first pressure parents of a child with Asperger Syndrome will face. There is the uncertainty, the practically having to jump through hoops to be seen by a doctor, the out-of-pocket expenses for testing, the feeling of being dismissed or thought to be over-reacting because you have concerns and, of course, the actual final diagnosis itself. To me, the worst part of the whole diagnosis process is the great sense of isolation that my husband and I felt. If your child was, God forbid, diagnosed with cancer, there would undoubtedly be an automatic all-encompassing support afterwards. Your family and friends understand the meaning of such a diagnosis. There is no need to have to explain; you can just concentrate on your child.

Now, I know that Autism is not a disease like cancer, and I certainly do not mean to downplay the horrific experience that would be. I am just trying to make the point that after you are finally given a name to these differences you have been noticing about your child, that's it. You are left on your own to find your way. Even when you try to reach out to your friends and family, they may not offer you the support you so desire and need. Heck, you probably don't even know what kind of support and help you need. And that is my argument: you get the diagnosis and then are left to figure out what to do, and that is a lot of pressure.

Dealing With the Diagnosis Pressure

So how do you deal with this? Simple. First, remember what the doctor whispered in my ear, "Your child is still the same person he was before he got the diagnosis." Don't think of the diagnosis as a label. Labels are for soup cans, and unless you named your kid Campbell's or Cup of Noodle, don't slap that label on him.

Asperger's is now a part of who your child is. Yes, it is a diagnosis, and to receive services, you will need that diagnosis. A diagnosis allows you to obtain tools and techniques; therapies and specialists who can help you help your child. It won't be easy to do because every child is different; therefore, what works for one may not work for another. Knowing this ahead of time will save you a lot of heartache later on. It will give you the strength to ignore the well-intended persons who will email the latest articles, which you have already read, and tell you what you should or should not do with your child. The best advice I can give you is to trust your gut and your child. Yes, take your cues from your child and BREATHE! Those first few months after a diagnosis – oh, heck, who am I kidding? – for years after the diagnosis you may need to be reminded to do this, so I will say it again… BREATHE!

Pressure #2: The Feeling of Being Judged

You are halfway through the grocery store and can tell that your Aspie is becoming tired, overstimulated and about to melt down. You know you should just 86 the whole thing and head out of Dodge before the gunfire explodes, but you really need milk, bread and coffee. (Got to have that coffee!) So you press on. Finally, your child cannot stand it anymore and falls to the floor in anger and frustration when you place a generic lemon-lime soda in the cart instead of the real deal SPRITE! The outside world sees a big sobbing and screaming kid having a fit similar to what they would expect from a two-year-old. You see the truth. Your baby has come apart, and you need to help put this little Humpty Dumpty back together again. But unlike the fairy tale, all the King's horses and all the King's men are not coming to help you out.

As you try to deal with the situation, by yourself, you can't help but feel the disapproving looks from the other shoppers. More than one nasty comment is made about how you need to maintain better control of your child or how spoiled he must be. You want to say something to these misinformed fools, but you do not have the time or energy to do so. Right now, you have to deal with your son and the reality that there will be no coffee, milk and toast in the morning.

Did the above scenario sound familiar? Almost every spectrum parent I have ever met has had this happen at least once. When it transpires, it leaves you angry, sad and perhaps even embarrassed. These complete strangers have judged you and accused you of being a bad mom or dad without knowing all the facts of the case. No matter how determined you are to not let it bother you, it does!

I wrote a post for my blog about one of these JUDGING moments that happened in physical therapy of all places back in May 2012. The post went viral, even crashing my server after getting close to 30,000 views in less than an hour. But instead of feeling happy that something I had written was so well received, it made me quite sad. You see, the 100 plus comments that followed the post confirmed what I already knew: we are constantly being judged.

In case you are wondering what I wrote in the post that resonated so much with the members of our community, here it is.

Dear Other Mother at Physical Therapy,

For the past three days I have watched you roll your eyes at my son. I can see your annoyance with him when he gets loud and interrupts your quiet, making it hard for you to read your book. I saw your anger when he accidentally bumped into you and just kept going instead of stopping to say he was sorry. I hear the hostility in your voice as you yell for the technicians to pay attention to your daughter and stop giving my boy extra attention. And for three days, I have said nothing.

I said nothing because, you see, I empathize with you. Who knows what has brought you to this place, but something happened that made your daughter hurt her leg. That incident may play over and over in your head and keep you up at night and, of course, make you irritable. Or maybe your daughter is the one waking up at night in pain from her hurt leg. How that must hurt you to see your child in pain, I know that hurt.

I said nothing because if there is one thing this journey I am on has taught me, it is to NOT JUDGE others. We do not know what others are really going through, and for this reason, I let it slide. BUT then it happened...

It happened as my boy was doing his exercises. To others it may have seemed like an easy task, but for my boy, walking around on his heels was anything but easy. Not only did this exercise cause him physical pain at the actual spot where they cut into his foot, but also, because it was a different sensation, his neurological system that is wired so differently from ours was definitely thrown out of whack. I watched my boy's face turn red and a rash break out on his forehead the way it always does when he is stressed. He was flapping his arms and doing whatever he could do to try to regulate himself. And then, he stopped in front of your daughter.

I watched my boy make direct eye contact with her, and without being prompted he said hello. I beamed with pride. Then it happened.

SHE ROLLED HER EYES and looked away from him.

My heart broke.

Thankfully, my boy did not notice. He just kept on doing his exercise, but I noticed...and so did you. I saw you watching your daughter as she did it, and you said nothing! You did not prompt her to be polite and say hello back; you let her dismiss my boy.

I do not blame your daughter's total disrespect for another human being. You see, she was only doing what she had observed. For three days as she sat back doing her own exercises, she watched you roll your eyes and get annoyed with him. She watched your lack of empathy and compassion. Of course this is how she would react.

I write this letter because, you see, I cannot afford to make a big deal out of this. I have to pick and choose my battles, and you, dear mother, even though it saddens me; you are not a battle I choose to fight.

I will write this letter and hope that some other mothers out there will read it and think about it. Perhaps the next time they feel like rolling their eyes when they see a boy like mine, perhaps they will remember this. Perhaps they will stop and think about who is around them, watching the way they are acting. And perhaps they will remember the golden rule and at least encourage their children to politely say hello back to my boy!

And when I see you and your daughter tonight or tomorrow or the next day at therapy, I will continue to be nice and encourage my boy to be the same. I will not judge you even though it would be easy to do. I will accept that we are just...DIFFERENT and pray that one day you will be able to do the same.

Signed,

The Mother of the Autistic Boy

Dealing with the Pressure of Being Judged

I know many folks who have business cards made up that state that their child has Autism and explain what it is. They feel that educating these judgmental, tisk-tisking, disrespectful types will help. My husband and I always joked that we were going to have our own cards made up that said, "My son has autism. He is not intentionally being naughty or rude, but you are!"

Of course, we never really did it, but wouldn't that be great to pass out...even just once. I can just see the look on that person's face. Priceless!

The bottom line is, "Haters gonna hate." I know I am lamely trying to sound like a teenage Facebook post, but there is some real wisdom in this. Judgmental people tend to judge. The time we spend getting people to stop judging is time away from being with our families or taking a few minutes to ourselves. People are going to do what they are going to do. I am becoming more and more able to push those that judge aside and not give them space in my head. I have enough going on in this bobble head of mine without clouding it up with thoughts of these folks who just don't matter.

Isn't there an old saying that goes something like, "Those that matter don't mind, and those that mind don't matter?" Choose to concentrate on those that matter!

Pressure #3: Financial Stress

There is a very special woman who I am fortunate enough to call my neighbor and friend. Her daughter and my Gracie are the same age, so we have much in common. You know the perils of raising TWEENS. We come from completely different backgrounds, yet the values we share are so similar you would think we were family. Although this particular pal does not have a special needs child, she has been around mine enough to understand what it is like. In fact, sometimes while we are talking, I forget that she is not an official member of the "club."

But inevitably, no matter how much I love this special lady, she will say something that will seem so foreign, so out of our family's reach, so "NORMAL," that I am snapped back into the reality of just how stressful and different our lives are. The other day this happened when she started talking about her daughter's college fund.

All the sudden I got this knot in the pit of my stomach. We have no college fund started for either of our children. Does this scare me? Heck yes! It is not that we don't want to do it, but there simply is no money left at the end of the day to start one.

I don't have to look at the most recent studies or research showing the astronomical cost of raising a special needs child. I am living it! We are fortunate, albeit sometimes I think unfortunate (I will explain that one in a minute), that Jay is able to attend a mainstreamed, very good public middle school. Of course to get him into this school system, we had to move into this school district. CHA-CHING! And here is the kicker. Because Jay, like many Aspies, is very intelligent and gets wonderful grades, he does not qualify for all services. You see, in order for a student to qualify for services, his disability has to directly affect his academics, which means that although my son, who is 12 years old and still has a hard time signing his own name in cursive, has the accommodation of having access to a computer, he does not qualify for any Occupational Therapy during school.

That means that we, the parents, have to seek it outside of school on our own. The same is true for social skill classes, physical therapy, a tutor to help him with the STRINGS instrument he is required to play, weighted blankets to help him sleep, fidgets to help him concentrate and the list goes on. I sat down the other day and calculated that our out-of-pocket expenses just for Jay last year were $6,345. That is one semester at public university tuition! And we have good insurance, live in a state that has health reform policies that cover the therapies we use and my son is not on any specific diet or medications. I cannot imagine how much we would pay if he was or if we did not have insurance.

Fortunately, I am able to write from home, allowing me the flexibility of being able to do what I need to do for my kids and contribute a little something to the household. Most families I know with a child on the spectrum have been forced to make the decision that one parent stay home. Someone has to be around to attend all those IEP meetings, fight with insurance companies and play taxi driver to therapy appointments.

Money does not solve all our problems, but I think I speak for most of us when I say it sure would be nice to have a little extra once in a while to see if that was true – or at least to start a college fund for my kids.

Dealing with Financial Pressures

Deal with present issues now. If that means that there is no money to put aside for college, then so be it. For someone who is a planner, this might be hard, but sometimes having faith that you will find a way to make things work when the time comes can be a big blessing.

There is a very real helplessness that a parent feels when he is unable to meet his child's needs because of finances. If your family is truly having a hard time making ends meet, there is no shame in asking for help. Fortunately, there are many nonprofits, social organizations and government agencies available to help should you need them. Examples of expenses for which you can request financial assistance are eyeglasses, adaptive car seats, compression garments and speech therapy. Some agencies may even pay a utility bill. Gather your paperwork: original bills, paycheck stubs, notes from hospitals or physicians. The paperwork can be overwhelming, but it's worth it. Below are some resources to help you get started with your research.

Aid for Autistic Children Foundation

aacfinc.org

The foundation's board and an independent consumer credit counseling service will evaluate your application and assist with debt relief. They deal directly with lien holders or carriers of your debt to "target the financial burden the family deems most obstructive in allowing them to focus solely on giving their autistic loved one the best tools and skills for a productive life in today's society."

AutismCares

www.autismcares.org

AutismCares is a consortium of leading autism organizations who have come together to support individuals with autism and their families during natural disasters and other catastrophic life events. They help families affected by autism cover costs associated with critical living expenses such as housing, utilities, car repair, daycare, funeral expenses and other essential items on a case-by-case basis.

United Healthcare Children's Foundation

www.uhccf.org

UHCCF provides individual grants for medical-related services and products, but only to individuals with private insurance.

Local service organizations might be able to provide money towards needed medical equipment or to help with bills. Examples of such organizations are Knights of Columbus, Rotary Club, the Shriners, Kiwanis International and Veterans' Groups. Social Security does not make it easy, but with persistence you may be able to qualify for help. You can also ask to speak with the social workers at your local children's hospital who may be aware of some type of grant or aid for which you and your family may qualify.

Most of the organizations I mentioned above are in need of donations so that they can continue to do the wonderful work they are doing. If you are in a position to help, please remember them. When your life levels out, see if you can support them with a local fundraiser and pay it forward.

Pressure #4: Mommy Guilt on Steroids

As I sit here writing this section, I cannot help but think about the mountain of clothes in the hallway that are not going to wash themselves, the breakfast dishes still sitting in the sink, the dog next to me whining to go out and the fact that I still need to change my clothes in order to go into the school in an hour to help with an Autism fundraiser that I initiated. There is a list of calls I need to return, emails I need to read and bills I need to pay. I feel torn between my need to write and finish this project, referred to as my baby by my kids (another thing that gives me guilt), and all the other duties that are piling up. In the back of my head, I am thinking that if I was a better mom, I would be able to do it all.

I have spent a good portion of my life feeling guilty. My husband says it is my Jewish background. Oy vey! Seriously, I cannot begin to tell you how many hours I have laid awake at night feeling guilty that I am not doing "this" right – "this" mothering thing, "this" wife thing, "this" writing a book thing and on and on and on. I know in my head that this type of thinking is unproductive, unhealthy, and every other UN word out there, yet I cannot help it.

And don't even get me started on the amount of time I wasted in the beginning of this journey with the whole "Was it something I did?" guilt! We won't go there now, but I know you understand what I am talking about.

One day, the realization hit me that most of my guilt comes out of the fact that I compare myself to other moms. I see the put-together, skinny mamas picking up their kids after school and feel guilty about the way I let myself go, yet I feel guilty if I take the time to go to the gym by myself. It's the vicious mommy guilt cycle of self-deprivation. It is the myth we all buy into when our babies are placed into our arms for the first time. Somehow we start to believe that being a good mommy means having to devote one's entire life to this child. No longer do we put our own needs first. We believe that being good mommies means losing our own identities and focusing completely on our kids. When we see another mother doing something we believe to be better than us, we feel guilty.

Mommy peer pressure = Mommy guilt on steroids.

How ironic is it that we constantly lecture our kids on peer pressure and yet give into it ourselves? "If your friend jumped off a cliff into shark infested water, would you jump too?" Ummm… yes, we do every day it seems. Except our sharks are wearing opaque liquid lipstick and carrying Dooney and Burke purses!

Dealing with Mommy Guilt

Mama guilt happens when we try to convince ourselves that we are good parents. The problem is that there is only one person who can accurately measure your performance: yourself! Comparing myself to others only makes me feel better or worse, depending on what mom I am comparing myself to. Instead, we need to concentrate on WHY we are doing something and make sure it is not related to showing others that we are good parents.

My biggest piece of advice is this: Don't let guilt drive your decisions. As I mentioned earlier, I feel guilty about letting my body go, and I feel guilty about going to the gym. If I am going to feel guilty regardless, what is the best choice for me? If I try to use guilt as the deciding factor, it won't work since I will feel guilty regardless of the decision.

Also, keep in mind the age-old adage: "If Momma ain't happy, then nobody's happy." If you don't do what you need to do to feel good about yourself, then it will affect both you and everyone around you.

Don't Freak Out

Chapter Four Summary

- Although we talk a lot about the pressures our Aspies feel, it is important to remember our own pressures.

- There are things you can do to decrease the parental pressures you are feeling. Consider trying one of the suggestions mentioned in this chapter.

Don't Freak Out Exercise

Sometimes we don't even realize how much stress and pressure we are feeling. Below is a quick little exercise you can use to see how stressed out you really might be feeling. Simply circle the number that indicates the level of pressure you are feeling when it comes to that topic, with 1 being "no sweat," 5 being "it's a good thing I am wearing deodorant" and 10 being "never mind deodorant; the veins in my forehead are about to explode!"

	No Sweat				Sweating it a bit			Vein Exploding		
Diagnosis	1	2	3	4	5	6	7	8	9	10
Being Judged	1	2	3	4	5	6	7	8	9	10
Financial	1	2	3	4	5	6	7	8	9	10
Mommy Guilt	1	2	3	4	5	6	7	8	9	10

How did you do? Do you have many that are 5 and above? That is a sure sign that you are over-pressured and feeling stressed out. Go back and reread the suggestions offered in this chapter.

Chapter 5
Parenting an Aspie and Marriage

I will never forget a conversation I had with an acquaintance shortly after receiving Jay's official diagnosis. The woman, who I assume was trying to be helpful, was asking how my husband and I were doing and if we were going to be okay. She then proceeded to tell me about an article she had read that stated that 85 to 90% of marriages with children on the spectrum ended in divorce. I smiled and assured her that WE were one of the 15% that would stay together and politely walked away from this Negative Nelly. Even so, I could not help but feel that I had just been given two diagnoses: A child with autism and a prediction for divorce.

Of course I went home and did my own research and never was able to find the report she spoke of. But for some reason, even today, this misconception of autism = divorce seems to exist. For couples who may already be experiencing stress in their marriage, there is no doubt that autism could be the proverbial straw that breaks the camel's back. But it doesn't have to be.

Take my marriage for example.

By all statistics, my husband and I should have called it quits a long time ago. We are an interfaith couple, one with a career in law enforcement, who met in a bar and are raising a child with special needs. Yet, we have weathered the storms, some of which were category 5 hurricanes mind you, and have been married for 14 years now. It got me thinking about what it really is that has kept us together when so many others have become victims to the "disability and divorce" syndrome. Then it hit me. The fact that we have a special needs child is what has made us stronger. Seriously, I honestly believe that the main reason we have and will continue to beat the odds (she says while knocking on wood and throwing salt over her shoulder) is that many of the techniques we use to deal with our son Jay are the same techniques we use with each other, and it works.

"I write as straight as I can, just as I walk as straight as I can, because that is the best way to get there." ~H.G. Wells

I also say exactly what I mean, too! With Jay you cannot assume that he will understand hidden context and pick up on body language or facial gestures. Beating around the bush just doesn't work. So, without realizing it, or perhaps we do realize it, my hubby and I communicate the same way. If I am angry, I don't huff and puff and sigh and hope he will figure out that I am upset over the dirty socks he left on the floor even though the hamper is a foot away. Nope, I tell him, "Can you please pick up your socks and put them in the hamper? And while you are there, why don't you throw a load of laundry in the machine. Thank you, sweetie!"

A compromise is an agreement whereby both parties get what neither of them wanted. ~Author Unknown

Like many people with the neurological disorder known as Asperger's, Jay can have a "my way or the highway" type behavior. It would be easy to get tough and lay down the law, so to speak, with him. I am sure he would comply, eventually, but there would be many tears and much frustration at first. Instead, I have learned to look at things differently, from all points of view, to give in a little bit on the things that really don't matter and only fight for those that really do. In other words, I have learned the art of compromise. Over the years I have learned to do the same with my marriage.

I think it is important to point out that there is a huge difference between compromise and constantly conceding. Conceding means giving up, and I certainly don't think that will work with our kids or our marriages. What I am talking about is learning to pick and choose your battles. As a parent of a child with special needs, I have learned that I just don't have the energy, patience and time to fight all battles. I am not conceding when I let my daughter walk out of the house wearing clothes I know do not match even if it is picture day. The picture will not even show her bottom half anyway. She was happy, and isn't that what really matters? I love my children and want them to be happy and to feel fulfilled and satisfied. I love my husband too and want him to feel the same way. In other words, some days instead of complaining about the smelly feet warmers (aka socks) on the floor, I will just bend down and pick the things up! Like the Scottish proverb goes: "Better bend than break."

"Men marry women with the hope they will never change. Women marry men with the hope they will change. Invariably they are both disappointed." ~Albert Einstein

I quote Albert Einstein... A LOT! Not only was he an incredible scientist who had wonderful insight into our human nature, but also, he is said to have had ASPERGERS! This particular quote is a favorite of mine. If there is one thing this roller coaster ride of Autism has taught me, it is that my boy is who he is. I don't need to change him. I just need to be his mom, to make him feel loved and accepted for the person he is now. I focus on now rather than what tomorrow may bring. I let him know TODAY how wonderful he is because I know in my heart if I do this today, tomorrow he will be even more wonderful.

I apply this same thinking to my husband. I may not like all the things he does, because you know he does not do them the way I would do them (which we all know is the right way), BUT, and that is a capitalized BUT not just a lower case one, I don't try to change him. I try to make him feel loved and accepted for the person he is now. I don't expect him to change his behaviors to conform to my way of thinking just as I don't expect my son or daughter to.

We tend to ask our spouses to change quite a bit. If only she would do what I ask her to, things would be better. If only he would scan the room before he leaves and picks up the plates and cups, things would be better. The problem is that most people tend to be a bit like Popeye: "I Yam What I Yam." They can change a little bit for a little while, but they tend to drift back to their natural ways of doing things. In a family with an Aspie, there tends to be someone who is more anxious and more focused on dealing with the extra responsibilities. Let's be honest and admit that nine times out of ten (at least), it's the mom who takes on the heavier load.

Does that mean that you should just accept things the way they are and not say anything? No. Neil says this is when the old elementary school "I messages" need to come out.

You don't remember learning about I messages? Sure you do. An "I message" as taught to kids, goes like this:

When you _____, I feel _____. Please _____.

For instance: "When you don't pick me during recess, I feel left out. Please pick me next time so that we can be on the same team."

For couples, Neil suggests the same idea but says to leave out the "Please do ____." At first, I too thought this was strange, but then Neil explained it to me this way, "The important part of being a couple is letting your spouse know how he is coming across to you. But when you tell him what you would like him to do, resistance begins to build. When you leave out the last sentence, you are telling your spouse, "This is how I am feeling about your actions (or inaction), but you get to decide what to do about it."

Neil often shares a really great story from his own marriage to explain this point even further. I am sure many of you might be able to see yourself and your loved one in it. Neil will be the first to tell you that he is not a very organized person. His wife Colleen, on the other hand, is very organized and naturally puts things back where they belong. For instance, Colleen usually takes off her shoes when she walks into their house and places them in one of the designated shoe baskets by the front door. Neil, on the other hand, tends to take his shoes off whenever and wherever he wants to relax, which is usually next to the couch. When he gets up from the couch to go somewhere else, his shoes tend to stay where they are.

Colleen would, from time to time, remind him to put his shoes in the basket. Neil would usually then say "OK" and put them in the basket. She hoped that if she told him a few times, he would remember and just start doing it. Of course, Neil didn't. Of course, Colleen got irritated. The angrier Colleen would get, the worse Neil got at putting his shoes away. He would get defensive in his mind, thinking, "Why does the neat person always win? It's my house too. I can leave my shoes wherever I want!"

(Are you seeing yourself in this scenario yet?)

One day during one of these indignant tirades that Neil was having in his head, Colleen came in very upset and said to him, "You don't get it, do you? When I come in from a hectic, tiring day, and see the house neat, it immediately calms me down. When I come home and see clutter, including your shoes next to the couch and newspapers lying around, it increases my stress."

That was all she said. She didn't tell Neil to clean up. She simply told him how she felt about the situation. Neil, of course, didn't want her to feel stressed. If he could make her feel better by putting stuff away, he would absolutely do that. It was a way he could show his love for her. The fact that she didn't tell him what to do made a big difference in helping Neil understand and act differently.

The moral of Neil's story? The next time your spouse is doing something that's bothering you, consider just letting him know how you feel instead of telling him what to do. You might be surprised at the response.

Don't Freak Out

Chapter Five Summary

- Even though there is no actual research or proof, the misconception of autism = divorce seems to exist.
- For couples who may already be experiencing stress in their marriages, there is no doubt that autism could be the straw that breaks the camel's back, but it doesn't have to be.
- Say exactly what you mean to your spouse; beating around the bush doesn't help. It will only make you more frustrated. Remember that there is no such thing as a mind reader.
- Accept your partner for who he is today, not who you hope he will become tomorrow.
- Use "I" messages: When you_____, I feel _____. Don't tell your partner what he should do. Let him make his own choices after hearing how you feel.

Chapter 6
The S.C.A.P.E Method

Well, here we are. You have made it this far and are ready to get to the meat and potatoes of this book. By now you have a better understanding of your Aspie and how he uses different styles to cope. You also understand what type of parent you are and how you can be a better leader for your child. Now, let's put this all together and use a simple acronym to help us remember.

When you are faced with a difficult situation – your child is about to meltdown, is getting upset over homework, is having a hard time sleeping or you are going through any other trying circumstances – remember:

S.C.A.P.E. Yes, I mean *scape* as in *landscape*, the whole big picture, not *escape*, hopping on your horse and heading out of Dodge.

S- Stay

C- Calm

The foundation of this method is remembering to stay calm – or at least doing your best to appear that way! Remember that old deodorant commercial with the tag line "Never let them see you sweat?" These are good words to live by when it comes to our Aspie kids. As discussed in Chapter 1, the calmer we are, the easier it is for our children to succeed.

A- Assess the Situation

This is where all the information you learned in chapter two comes in handy. It will help you gather some objective data to assess the situation instead of just relying on your own emotions to make the assessment. Is he being a Rule Follower? Does he seem Anxious? Is there a hint of analytical reasoning going on? Does he want to lose himself in a fictional world? Is he being a Debbie Downer, Negative Nancy, Pessimistic Pete or Grumpy Gus? Look behind the tears and angry words and get to the bottom of his actions so that you can react appropriately.

P- Pick a Parenting Style

Remember: this book is not about changing your Aspie; it's about changing the way you parent your Aspie. Once you have an idea as to why your child is using the coping style he is using, then you can choose which parenting style might work best. Of course, the first parenting style is the Calm Parent style, so we won't include that one here. The three parenting styles we would like you to choose from are the Supporter, the Consultant and the Boss. (Go back to Chapter 3 if you need to review them.) Here is a cheat sheet as to which of the three may be most useful with each Aspie coping style. No two Aspies are alike, so you may need to play around with these styles to see which works best.

Aspie Style	First Try	Maybe Try
Rule Follower	Consultant	Boss
Anxious	Supporter	Consultant
Analytical	Boss	Consultant
Fictional World	Supporter	Boss
Doom, Gloom	Supporter	Boss

To help you better understand this, I will recount a few examples used in chapter two. This time I will highlight how the best leadership style could have worked.

The Rule Follower- Remember the pretzels at the water park episode I had with Jay? A Consultant style approach to that would have been to stand beside Jay as he was examining the sign and calmly say, "Yes, Jay, you are correct. The sign does say that we are not supposed to bring in outside food. Why do you think it says that?" To which my boy most likely would have said very matter-of-factly, "Because they want you to buy from the snack bar." I could have then offered him something to think about by saying, "So, if we bought something from the snack bar, do you think it would be so bad if we also had a little something that we brought in that the snack bar does not offer? After all, we sometimes do that when we go to other places, bring snacks that you like when we know the place does not have them. Those places usually do not mind because we are still supporting them." Would he have been more agreeable? Most likely, yes.

The Analytical Aspie- The example I used for this one was when Jay was stuck, unable to go down the zipline because he was too busy trying to logically figure out every detail and every possibility from every angle. Finally, my husband stepped up and used the Boss Leadership role by telling Jay to stop thinking and just do it. So Jay did it and still talks about the feeling of soaring through the trees to this day. Sometimes the Boss style can be used to help our kids, especially our Analytical Aspies, get unstuck.

The Doom, Gloom and Boom Aspie- The example I will use to show how the Supporter can be effective is the incident when Jay lost his pencil and told his classmates that if it was not returned by the end of the day, he would rip their heads off. Jay was angry and depressed. Simply telling him that I was sorry for his loss calmed him down. I validated his feelings. I supported him. He no longer needed to fight because he finally felt someone was on his side and understood his very real grief.

Remember: the purpose is not to change our children. It is to understand them better and to calmly lead them in the right direction. Knowing when to use the Consultant, the Boss, and the Supporter may be confusing at first. I suggest taking your cues from your Aspie. They are constantly communicating with us, just not always with their words.

E- Evaluate Effectiveness

Is it working? Do I need to try a different parenting style? Did I perhaps miss something and not assess my child accurately? Just as we suggest that our kids double check their answers when they finish a test in two minutes, we need to double check our parenting styles.

These are not just parenting styles. They are leadership styles. The goal is to lead your child into making better choices or figuring out calming techniques on his own. Like anything else, this is a new way of thinking and acting. Change is hard, and you may not see the results you are hoping for right way. Be persistent, and try a method for at least three weeks. Our Aspies are smart, sometimes too smart. Most likely they will be thinking something like this:

- Week One: "I guess she read a new parenting book. Here we go again. I'll just wait her out."

- Week Two: "This is getting pretty tiring. She usually gives up by now. Let me wait a little longer."

- Week Three: "I think she means it. She is not giving up."

Your mileage may be different, but I am suggesting three weeks so that you don't give up too quickly. Some Aspies may respond very well right away, and other more persistent and defiant children may require five or six weeks. I know that seems like a long time, but the longer you try a proven technique, the greater the chance that it will be effective. When we go back and try to measure effectiveness of a new technique, it is easy to focus on our children. It is so important to remember that we are not trying to change them. The only person you can change is yourself, so you need to concentrate on numero uno…you!

First, ask yourself…

Did I remain calm? Many times we think we are being calm when in reality we are not. This might be a good time to ask for the opinion of someone else (not your kids) who can be honest about how calm you actually are. Our Aspies might not be great on picking up on certain nonverbal communication, but for some reason this one they definitely get right away. A few nonverbal ways to "yell" without raising your voice are:

- Glaring

- Finger Pointing

- Head Shaking

- Foot Tapping

- Exaggerated Sighing

- Crossing of Arms

If you think you might be coming across as angry, enlist the help of another who can observe while you deal with your child during a difficult situation.

The good news is that most Aspies crave routine and structure, and the S.C.A.P.E. method certainly will give you a more structured way of parenting. It may not be easy at first, but your kids are certainly worth it.

Don't Freak Out

Chapter Six Summary

- When you are experiencing a difficult situation with your child such as a meltdown, remember the acronym S.C.A.P.E.
- Stay Calm, Access the situation, Pick a Parenting style, Evaluate the Effectiveness.
- There are only three effective ways to lead your Aspie child through a difficult situation. Your task is to choose carefully which one will work the best: the Supporter, the Consultant or the Boss.

Chapter 7
Early Interventions and Treatments

"A treatment method or an educational method that will work for one child may not work for another child. The one common denominator for all of the young children is that early intervention does work, and it seems to improve the prognosis." – Temple Grandin

If you had a child with vision problems, including blindness, wouldn't you give that child all of the tools you could to help him function better in society? You would seek to provide glasses so that he could see the world more clearly, teach him Braille so that he could read or provide him with a Seeing Eye dog to guide him safely through obstacles. If your child was hard of hearing, I am sure that you would fit him for hearing aids or teach him to read lips and use sign language to communicate with others. In my opinion, this is what early interventions and treatments should be about. The earlier the diagnosis, the quicker we can know what tools our children need to help them navigate through childhood and the rest of their lives. It is not so that we can change them, for this is who they are. Autism is just as much a part of your child's genetic makeup as the color of his eyes.

Our job as parents of any child is to create a safe, loving atmosphere filled with all of the tools our children need to help them grow, develop and mature into adults who not only function in society but also hopefully contribute in a way that will make it better. Your child has Asperger's, but your goal is the same as any other parent. Sure, he may have more challenges than others, but that just means that he needs access to more tools than others might. It does not mean that the end goal is any different!

In this chapter we will talk about some of these tools (also referred to as treatments or techniques), their purposes and the pros and cons of each. As we have mentioned many times before, it is important to remember that every child is different and unique, so finding the methods that work best for that child is key. Some of the therapies we will discuss are supported by years and years of research while others, well, not so much. Children under the age of three may qualify for some of the Early Childhood Intervention programs that are federally funded by the Individuals with Disabilities Education Act (IDEA). School-age kids may qualify for therapy in the public school setting, also in accordance with IDEA. While other therapies we will mention will require private funding, I must warn you that it can be quite expensive and time consuming.

Read through these brief descriptions and then get out your cap and pipe because it will be time to play Sherlock Holmes and perform your own investigation. Be sure to choose professionals who have the skill, experience and personality that will best suit your child. A good rule of thumb to remember is that an effective treatment program is one that includes the parent, builds on the child's interest, promotes self-esteem and addresses your youngster's weaknesses while first and foremost focusing on their strengths! I think I will repeat that because, well, it is worth repeating. First and foremost, concentrate on your child's strengths.

I personally would not and do not contemplate any treatments or interventions with my son that I would not consider using on my neurotypical daughter as well. Before engaging in any intervention technique, I ask myself these questions:

- What is the goal behind this treatment?
- Is this treatment individualized for my child?
- By accepting this treatment, what message am I sending to my child?
- How will this message affect my child's self-image, self-esteem?
- Is this the message that I want my child to carry with him, to internalize, to take into adulthood?
- Am I doing this because it will benefit my child or because I feel the need to do "something"?
- How much does this cost?
- What are the possible side effects?

If I can answer these questions favorably, if this is something I would do even if my child did not have Asperger's, if this will give my boy the tools he needs to help him overcome some of his challenges, if I am truly doing this for him and not just because my neighbor did it and it worked for her child, then this might be the right intervention for Jay.

Here is a Cheat Sheet (in alphabetical order) of the 10 most common therapies/interventions we will be discussing.

Types of Therapy	Goal	Age Group
(ABA)Applied Behavioral Analysis	Basic cause-and-effect learning	Early intervention
(CBT) Cognitive Behavioral Therapy	Appropriate behavioral responses by reducing Negative feelings	Childhood, adolescence, adulthood
Floortime	Encourage social development skills	Early intervention
Gluten-Free, Casein-Free Diet	Eliminate gastric problems	Childhood, adolescence
Occupational Therapy (OT)	Fine motor skills, sensory processing	All
Pharmacological Treatments	Maximize independence and learning, decrease maladaptive behaviors	Older childhood & beyond
Physical Therapy (PT)	Improve gross motor skills, balance and coordination	All
Social Skills Training	Improving social skills, communication and behavior	All
Speech Therapy	Verbal and nonverbal communication	All
Therapeutic animals	Sensory, emotional	All

(ABA)Applied Behavioral Analysis

ABA is a behavior-modification approach to learning based on the work of Dr. B.F Skinner. Skinner believed that behaviors can be increased or decreased depending on the consequence the behavior receives. In other words, if a specific behavior is reinforced, there is an increased likelihood of that behavior occurring again in the future. While some therapies focus on the emotional roots of unwanted behaviors, applied behavior analysis focuses on the behaviors themselves. This approach to behavioral therapy has received much praise and criticism alike.

Pros

This method requires strong parenteral involvement, and the therapists are required to keep extensive notes. Many studies and much research have been done on this method.

Cons

Research indicates that in order for this method to be the most effective, 40 hours a week of therapy is required. This is extremely time consuming and costly. Opponents to this method claim that ABA produces robotic-like children who do not think independently.

Cognitive Behavioral Therapy

Cognitive-behavioral therapy (CBT) was established in the 1960's by Dr. Aaron Beck for the treatment of depression. Since then, CBT has been proven effective in the management of a wide variety of conditions in which emotion and/or behavior dysfunction is a core symptom. It is extremely effective in helping Anxious Aspies and/or the Doom, Gloom and Boom Aspies. CBT is a goal-oriented, skills-based intervention that focuses on the connection between thoughts/feelings (i.e., *cog-*

nitions) and actions (i.e., *behaviors*). CBT teaches how to change negative thoughts into positive ones so that the individual can feel better and therefore is able to react in a healthy manner.

Pros

Since many of our Aspies are logical and thought-oriented rather than emotional thinkers, this form of therapy usually is very effective. It is a structured therapy, which is also why it seems to be effective with people with Asperger's. It is a quick therapy that usually produces quick results. Many insurance companies will cover this as it performed via a Psychotherapist.

Cons

Some people feel this is a Band-Aid or quick fix therapy that does not address the underlying problem. It also only works if the Aspie is willing to allow it. If the Aspie does not see the therapist as a trustworthy and knowledgeable expert who truly cares about him, no amount of sessions will get the Aspie to change his thinking and thus correct the behavior in question.

Floortime

Floortime is a type of Early Intervention therapy developed by Dr. Stanley Greenspan to help children with special needs learn to interact with the people and objects in their world. It is used in a variety of ways to work on everything from sensory issues to speech and language.

Pros

It is a relatively low cost therapy as parents can buy a book or video and then just get down on the floor with their child and start right away.

Cons

It requires a lot of patience, imagination and stamina. In addition, since there is very little in the way of specific direction (each child is different), it can be difficult to know if you're engaging in the therapy properly and effectively.

Gluten-Free Casein-Free Diet

The Gluten-Free and Casein-Free (GFCF) Diet involves eliminating gluten and casein from your Aspie's diet. Gluten and casein are both naturally occurring proteins. Gluten is found in wheat, barley and rye while casein is found in dairy products like milk, cheese and yogurt.

Pros

The benefit of a gluten-free/casein-free diet is based on the theory that autistic individuals may have an allergy or high sensitivity to foods containing gluten or casein. According to the theory, processed peptides and proteins in foods containing gluten and casein affect people with autism differently than those without autism. Those that are in favor of this diet believe that this difference in processing may exacerbate gastrointestinal issues. Many parents believe that the GFCF Diet greatly improved their child's gastric symptoms, behavior, sleep and even communication skills.

Cons

To date, there is no concrete medical evidence that this diet works. Furthermore, removing gluten and casein from your diet is difficult, expensive and in some cases risky. Eliminating gluten may cause loss of fiber, vitamins and minerals, and a casein-free diet may contribute to calcium and vitamin D deficiencies that lead to decreased bone development and an increased risk of broken bones in children.[1] As with any diet program, you should consult a physician before starting it.

Occupational Therapy (OT)

Of the different types of therapy, occupational therapy is one of the more practical and understandable therapies from which a child with Asperger's can benefit. Some children with Asperger's have trouble with fine motor skills, which prevents them from mastering self-care activities such as buttoning their pants, tying their shoes or even brushing their own teeth. OT can help with these types of fine motor skills in addition to handwriting and even sensory issues.

Pros

The OT will evaluate the child and develop an individualized treatment plan specific to that child. Specific goals relate to activities that directly affect the child's day-to-day operations. Mastering a skill such as being able to zip a jacket will not only take some stress off you as the parent, but also, it will do wonders for your child's self-esteem and move him closer to independence.

Cons

It is actually rather difficult to think of cons for OT as most insurance companies do cover it. Perhaps one con would be that many people have to wait a long time before they can undergo their initial evaluation and begin therapy.

Pharmacological Treatments

There is an enormous debate over the use of medications with our kids. I think it is important to point out that there is no drug for Asperger's. When drugs are used, they are prescribed to treat underlying conditions or parallel diagnoses such as ADHD, anxiety or depression. It is important to weigh the benefits against the possible side effects your child could experience while taking the medication.

Pros

Many parents swear that without drugs their children would be unable to focus or suffer from panic attacks or violent episodes. These parents view the use of medication as a means of getting back the child they know and love.

Cons

Many people view pharmacological treatments as an easy fix. It is like putting a Band-Aid on a deep cut. It might hold things together at first, but eventually you are going to need stitches. Finding the right "cocktail" of drugs is very complicated. One medicine usually leads to another medicine. For example, a drug prescribed to deal with hyperactivity may cause insomnia which would require a different medication. Another con is that medications need to be taken every day, usually at the same time each day, which can be difficult with children. Certain medications may not be covered under your insurance, and these drugs are not cheap.

Physical Therapy (PT)

An awkward gait and lack of balance are common complaints of many folks with Asperger's. Physical therapy may help your youngster learn to kick a ball, walk up and down stairs and ride a bicycle.

Pros

Physical therapy can improve strength and range of motion and can teach your child ways to relieve muscle pain (stretching etc.).

Cons:

PT is therapist driven, which means that, if you work with a therapist who does not understand Asperger's, he may not recognize when your child is frustrated or needs exercises and directions to be broken down into small steps.

Social Skills Training

Our success in life relies greatly on how well we are able to interact with others. For our Aspies, social skills usually learned through observation alone do not come easy. This is where social skills training comes in. Since social skills are best taught in social situations, most training is done in groups. The groups are made up of a professional who is the leader/coach as well as students and peers who have already mastered the skills. Social stories, role- playing and games are used to help teach the concepts.

Pros

Skills are introduced in a safe environment where the child can make a mistake and receive corrective feedback immediately and in a positive manner. With repetition, practice and support the students' gain mastery and confidence and are more comfortable interacting with others in their everyday lives.

Cons

Social skills training is not like dog training. You can't simply say "sit" and then hand over a dog treat. Much patience is needed, and the Aspie must be willing to do the homework. Also, many Aspies can become frustrated as they don't understand why they must be the ones to conform to everyone else. "Why is my way always the wrong way?" they may think. In order for social skills training to work, it is essential that those with Asperger's knows that we are not trying to change who they are; we are just offering them more tools so that they can deal with the mostly neurotypical world around them.

Speech Therapy

Some parents are confused when speech therapy is suggested for their Aspies. Kids with Asperger's may be verbally gifted but tend to have pragmatic language concerns. They may not understand how to take turns during a conversation, may stand too close to people when talking, may have difficulty understanding nonverbal cues or facial expressions or may be extremely literal and unable to pick up on sarcasm or idioms. Speech therapy can help with all of this as well as with intonation, getting rid of a robotic-like speech pattern, and with low oral muscle tone, which can interfere with chewing and eating.

Pros

Speech therapy is highly individualized and specific goal-oriented. It helps to make the child more aware and less uncomfortable about being in social settings, thereby increasing self-confidence and self-esteem.

Cons

Insurance may or may not cover this therapy, and chances are that your child will not qualify for speech as part of his IEP in a public school setting. Also, you may have to travel a great distance or wait a long time to see a speech therapist who has experience dealing with Asperger's.

Therapeutic Animals

Research into animal-assisted therapy is fairly new. However, even among professionals who believe more research is in order, there's a general consensus that therapy animals can be a highly beneficial addition to treatment programs for children with Asperger's. Animal-assisted therapy can be as simple as bringing a family pet into the household or as structured as a program that offers horseback riding or swimming with dolphins.

Pros

Interacting with animals can help Aspies improve their strength, coordination and physical abilities. More importantly, the relationship formed with animals can help children develop a better sense of well-being, enhance their self-confidence and offer transferable skills of empathy and relating to others.

Cons

Animals can be extremely unpredictable, and many kids with Asperger's crave certainty and structure. As an example, a child who has sensitive hearing could become overly stimulated when a dog barks.

Take Your Cues from Your Child

The most important thing I believe you need to keep in mind when considering any treatment is to take your cues from your child. When they are ready to do something, believe me, they will do it. I know because my Jay, at the age of 12, ate TOAST. I know that may not seem like book-worthy info, but it will when I explain.

When Jay was three years old, he attended speech therapy, not because he was delayed in speaking, but because he would only eat five different foods. While Jay loved his physical and occupational therapists, he hated his speech therapist. I thought it was because she was forcing him to try new things and that if he continued to meet with her, he would learn to love her. Besides, he needed this, I thought; what choice did we have?

One day, I picked up my generally happy boy from preschool, ready to take him to therapy, and noticed he had a piece of tape over his mouth. The teacher quickly explained that he had done this when she told him to pack his bag. When she asked him why he took the tape from her desk and did that, he responded, "So I don't have to try new foods." I eventually convinced him to take the tape off by telling him that he did not have to eat the foods. I just wanted him to smell them, touch them, maybe just put it in his mouth and spit it out. My thinking was that this would be a start, and this was exactly what I told the therapist when I saw her. She told me not to worry, that they were only going to try plain toast and that everyone LOVES toast once they taste it. She enticed Jay into the room by telling him she was going to teach him the "Yeah Toast" song and dance. My boy left my side with a look of concern. I felt the need to go with him, but the therapist assured me it was just TOAST with not even a dab of butter on it. He would be fine.

I played with baby Gracie in the waiting room, trying to hear what was happening in the other room. Suddenly, a crazy sounding song could be heard. The baby laughed and giggled, I laughed and giggled, Jay cried! The door flew open, and Jay ran into my arms saying, "No toast!" The therapist came rushing out, shaking her head. "I don't understand," she said. "I have never seen any child refuse to eat toast like that. He is very defiant. If you don't do something, you will always have problems with him. Why don't you join us, and we will try again?"

I looked down at my boy who was hugging my leg. I bent down and held his chubby, precious face between my two palms and asked him what the problem was. "I am not ready to try toast, Mama! No Yeah Toast!" And with that, it all suddenly made sense. I did not care what the so-called experts said we should do or not do. From that point on, I was going to take my cues from my boy. He would do things on his agenda, when he was ready. Somehow I just knew this about my child. So, I put the baby back in her stroller, grabbed Jay's hand and started walking towards the door.

Just as we were about to exit the door, the therapist asked if we would be back. I turned around and simply said, "No Yeah Toast!" We found a different therapist that understood and never, ever tried to make my baby eat toast or anything else if he did not want to.

Here we are, nine years later, and honestly I had forgotten all about that day until a few weeks ago when my son asked me for toast during breakfast. My heart skipped a beat when he asked. I guess he thought I did not hear him because he asked again. "I think I would like to try a piece of toast with my eggs today, Mom. It is part of a well-balanced breakfast you know. Just plain toast though, and please don't toast it too much, okay?" As I put the toast in the toaster, making sure it did not get too done, all the memories of that day so many years ago came flooding back. With a tear in my eye, I handed my son his breakfast and then sat down with him. I wondered how much he remembered from that day so long ago but was afraid to ask. I did not need to because after he took a bite, he put his thumb up and said, "Yeah Toast!" I ran over to the computer and found the Yeah Toast! song, and the two of us danced in the kitchen, laughing hysterically.

My boy ate toast, on his own time, his way. That is definitely book worthy! Yeah Toast!

[1] Hediger ML, England LJ, Molloy CA, Yu KF, Manning-Courtney P, Mills JL (2008). "Reduced bone cortical thickness in boys with autism or autism spectrum disorder". *J Autism Dev Disord* **38** (5): 848–56.

 ## *Don't Freak Out*
Chapter 7 Summary

Get out your cap and pipe and investigate as if you were Sherlock Holmes. Ask yourself these questions:

- What is the goal behind this treatment?
- Is this treatment individualized for my child?
- By doing this, what message am I sending to my child?
- How will this affect my child's self-image, self-esteem?
- Is this the message that I want my child to carry with him, to internalize, to take into adulthood?
- Am I doing this because it will benefit my child or because I feel the need to do "something"?
- How much does this cost?
- What are the possible side effects?

Chapter 8
The School Years

"We all have our own life to pursue, our own kind of dream to be weaving, and we all have the power to make wishes come true, as long as we keep believing." ~Louisa May Alcott

When Jay was in 5th grade, his art teacher called me at home one day and asked if I could come in to help because they were starting weaving – well, more like coiling – baskets, and she said it would be challenging. I took that to mean that she thought Jay could become frustrated, and she would be grateful for my help. I appreciated the call and, even more so, the fact that this teacher was thinking ahead about my boy and what might "challenge" him.

When I arrived the next day, Jay's class was already sitting on the floor around the art teacher, who sat in the middle on a chair with a bunch of baskets at her feet. Each child had a plastic bag filled with all of the materials they would need to get started. She was going over instructions. The children stared up at her with blank faces, all of them confused by the multitude of steps she was cruising through. Jay was in the back, playing with his yarn. I guess the teacher noticed me looking at him because she then made a point of having Jay move closer.

"Jay, why don't you move over here in front so you can see me better," she said.

"How do I get over there?" he replied, obviously already becoming emotional and frustrated.

The teacher looked at him confused. To her, it was very clear that all he needed to do was get up and walk around the other students and work his way to the front of the group. I could see her getting frustrated with him. Jay could too.

I wiggled my way over to Jay and whispered to him, *"Jay, how do you get from point A to point B? You are at Point A. She wants you to sit in front of her, which is Point B. GO!"* My very logical problem-solving boy smiled, thought for a second and then moved all of the way to the back of the room so that he could walk around the perimeter until he made his way to the front where he sat down. It certainly was not the most direct route or quickest path, nor was it the road I would have taken, but he made it to point B. Mission accomplished. I gave him the thumbs up sign. He smiled contently.

The teacher continued on with the very complicated instructions and then dismissed the kids and sent them back to their tables to try to duplicate what she had just demonstrated. Jay sat there on the floor frozen in fear. I pulled him to his feet and led him to a table in the back of the room. I knew something else was up. As soon as we sat down, Jay began to cry, *"I forgot to do my study guide, I didn't have you sign my agenda, and now this?"*

I looked him in the eye and said, *"Jay, first off, breathe! We all forget things. It's okay. It's part of being human. You got to let that go. You made a mistake, and now we move on. And as far as this weaving thing goes...heck, I am overwhelmed by it to. But we can try to figure it out together. That is all I ever ask of you, Jay – that you try."* My son smiled at me and then said, *"Coiling!"* I looked at him, confused, so he continued. *"It's coiling a basket Mom, not weaving!"* And we were back in business!

As I helped my boy loop and "coil," stitch and turn, it donned on me how much our life is like this. When coiling a basket, you constantly have to pull it together and keep it tight, or else the foundation will have a hole, and, well, everything will fall out of your basket. That is what we do. We are constantly turning, readjusting and doing whatever we need to do to keep everything tight so that nothing – especially our children – falls through the holes in the middle.

As parents, we need to work with the schools, teachers, administrators, therapists and, of course, our children themselves to make sure they get from Point A to Point B. It doesn't matter how they get there, how long it takes or if it is the path that you or I would have taken. It just matters that they find their way there. Their job is to travel the road; our job is to do whatever we can to make sure that their path is as free from potholes as it possibly can be. Since a pothole is bound to occur sooner or later, our job is to also make sure our kids know how to fix the inevitable flat tires that come with life.

This chapter deals with school. We will talk about inclusive classroom environments, IEPs vs. 504s, home-to-school communication logs, transitioning from elementary school to middle and, of course, the ever-dreaded puberty phase. More importantly, we will talk about your role as a parent in all of this.

Your Role as a Parent in Creating an Inclusive Classroom Environment

"Wait a minute", you might be saying. "I am not an educator; I know nothing about teaching. How am I supposed to help create an inclusive classroom? What is an inclusive environment anyway?" Great questions. I will do my best to answer them.

The Individuals with Disabilities Education Act (IDEA) mandates not only that individuals with disabilities should be provided a public education, but also, that they have the right to learn in the least restrictive environment. This means that students with disabilities, both in public and in private schools, are, to the maximum extent possible, to be educated in classrooms alongside students without disabilities, but an inclusive classroom is more than your Aspie just being in a-so called mainstream or general education class with other non-Aspies.

Inclusion is being a part of what everyone else is doing. It is about creating an environment where everyone feels welcomed and as though they belong. It is an acceptance of diversity, a sense that there is no need to conform in order to be accepted. Inclusion classrooms allow our Aspies to go to school with their neighbors, friends and peers while still receiving whatever specially-designed instruction and support they may need in order to achieve high standards and succeed as learners. It is the ideal environment in which we want all of our children to be taught, whether they have special needs or not.

Creating this type of environment for your child is not just the teacher's responsibility, it's yours too. You know your child better than anyone. You know what makes him tick, what sets him off, what calms him. By sharing your knowledge, your resources and your time with the teacher, you can help to create the best possible learning environment for your child. Perhaps you are not sure how to do this. Let me give you a few suggestions.

1. Before school starts, create a binder about your child for the teacher(s)

Don't assume that the teacher has read all the reports or your child or that she has talked to last year's teachers. This is not the time to write a novel. Keep it short, to the point and easy to read.

The first page should be a thank you note to the teacher, letting her know how excited you are to work with her this year and introducing yourself and your child in addition to providing your contact information.

The second page should describe all the wonderful, GOOD qualities of your child: how creative he is, how he excels in science, how he follows rules etc. Too often we start off with the challenges. This teacher may not know your child, so why not start off by telling her how exciting it is going to be to have him in class and all the great things he will offer rather than starting the conversation with a list of challenges

On the third page, you can take the time to discuss some of your child's challenges and strategies that have worked in the past. After that you can include resources or copies of articles that may be helpful to the teacher, perhaps a copy of the communication log (we will get to that a little later in this chapter) and a copy of the IEP. Many times the teacher will not receive the actual IEP until after school starts. This will help the teacher and will be something that she can refer to easily at a later time. Take your nice binder and perhaps a plate full of cookies or some chocolates and deliver your gifts to the school office/teacher's mailbox the week before school is to start. The sweet treats are a nice touch and a surefire way to make sure the teacher will at least take a peek in the binder.

NOTE - I also have Jay write what we call a One-Pager, which he gives to the teachers himself. The reality is that teachers are busy. They may not get to your BINDER of info right away, but they will most definitely read a One-Pager that is handed to them by the student. (It would be kind of rude if they didn't.) Below is a copy of the most recent One-Pager Jay wrote and then passed out to all his 7ᵗʰ grade teachers. This is a huge step towards helping my boy become his own self advocate. You can find a wonderful video as well as a template at the I Am Determined website. (See the resource section in the back of this book for the web address.)

MY LIKES ARE...		MY STRENGTHS ARE...
Comic Books		Math
Chess		Science
Sci Fi (but not Star Trek)		Chess
Doctor Who		And being Witty and Funny
Riddles		
Starburst Candy addiction		

MY NEEDS ARE...

I need to be able to use the computer to type anything more than two paragraphs.

I need copy of notes as I cannot always read the ones I take.

I think in pictures so I need to see things to get it.

If I tell you I need a break, please let me so I don't have a meltdown in front of my peers.

I need to be reminded to not blurt out answers.

MY PREFERENCES ARE...

I prefer to sit in the front of the class and close to someone I know.

I prefer being talked to in a calm demeanor because I get stressed easy and if you are yelling it will stress me out.

I prefer having someone be in front of me when they talk to me so I stay focused on what they are saying.

THINGS THAT STRESS ME OUT (but I am working on)...

When things change(like substitute teachers or a fire drill that I don't know about); when I get a bad grade, when I don't get something right away that others get, when others don't follow the rules, loud noises, bright lights, being forced to do something I don't really like.

2. Meet with the teacher

Your introduction letter should include that you would love to meet with her before school starts so that you can brainstorm and figure out the best way for the two of you to communicate, ensuring that everyone is on the same page when it comes to your child. I always throw in there, "Hey, if you try something and it is working at school, I want to know so we can try it at home! And vice a versa of course." Saying this lets the teacher know that I am willing to accept new ideas and that I hope she will be too. It lets her know that you are not just a bystander but an active participant in your child's education.

3. Help and Support the Teacher

This may mean going into the classroom and helping with other children so that the teacher is free to help yours. If you are a working parent, it could simply mean offering to do things at home. You would be amazed how helpful it is to your teacher to have assistance cutting out 100 leaves for the Tree of Thanks project. I know that, as special needs parents, we are already overtaxed, but so is your child's teacher. If lending a hand will give her extra minutes to spend with your child, it's worth it!

4. Offer feedback

We all are really quick to send an email when something is not working, but why not let the teacher know when something is! Teachers are human, and we all like to feel appreciated and as though what we do matters. Don't wait until Teacher Appreciation Day to let them know how grateful you are. Of course if something is not working, they need to know, but it is always nice to start even those emails with an encouraging comment when you can.

If we want our children to be in a loving, nurturing environment, then we need to be willing to do what we can to make that happen.

IEPs and 504s

Remember when I talked in the last chapter about our job being to give our children all the tools they need to be successful? Well, for many of our kids, that will include getting them the modifications and accommodations they need to succeed in school. In order to get these, you are most likely going to need an IEP or 504. I keep throwing around these terms, and perhaps you are not yet familiar with them. Don't worry. I am going to give you a quick and easy crash course on what they are and the differences between the two. Ready? Here we go.

First off, you should know that all children ages 3-22 in the Unites States are entitled to a Free and Appropriate Public Education (known as FAPE), which is outlined under the federal regulations of the Individuals with Disabilities Education Act (IDEA). All states are required to follow IDEA, and some states and districts even have additional laws to benefit children with disabilities. While you will need to check with your state and school district to see what services are available and who qualifies, the following is a pretty good representation of what is usually the norm.

Let's begin with a 504 plan, also known as Section 504, which is an anti-discrimination, civil rights statute that requires the needs of students with disabilities to be met as adequately as the needs of the non-disabled. Basically, this statute seeks to level the playing field so that students with disabilities can safely pursue the same opportunities as everyone else. A 504 is for the child who has a physical or mental impairment that substantially limits major life activities. Major life activities include caring for ones' self, performing manual tasks, walking, seeing, hearing, speaking, breathing, learning and working. A child with a 504 may or may not have a formal diagnosis. Modifications and accommodations under 504 usually refer to improving building accessibility, classroom accommodations and curriculum modifications. Here are a few examples:

- Annie has diabetes. Twice a day she will go to the nurse's office to have her glucose levels checked. She will be allowed snacks at any time if necessary.

- Zach has ADHD. His seat will be in the front, he will be given extra time for writing and homework assignments and he will receive weekly reports to monitor progress.

- Joey has severe asthma. He will be allowed to carry his own inhaler and administer the medication if needed. He will have a locker that is centralized and free of atmospheric changes. He will be allotted rest periods and modified physical education. The school will develop an emergency plan of action and will modify its attendance policy due to excessive absence because of his condition.

An IEP, or Individualized Education Plan, falls under the Individuals with Disabilities Education Act and is much more concerned with education. Students who qualify for an IEP generally require more than just a leveling of the playing field. They require educational assistance or remediation and are more likely to work on their own level at their own pace. To qualify for an IEP, the child must have a disability, AND it must affect his educational progress. Jay, for example, qualifies for an IEP because his test scores show that he is gifted and should be able to take honors classes, but in order to do that, he will need some accommodations and modifications. With these special education services in place, Jay is able to obtain the educational progress he is capable of achieving.

I know it can seem confusing, so I simplify it in my head and think of the two in this way:

- A 504 <u>removes barriers</u> to foster equality.
- An IEP <u>adds services</u> to foster equality.

Here is a chart to help you better understand the differences between the two:

504	IEP
Offers ALL children with disabilities equal access to education	Only for children who require special education services
No specific timelines or individualized goals	Very specific timelines, objectives and goals
The school staff member uses a check list of available accommodations.	The document must address each child's individual needs.
No required parental involvement. Also no requirements stating who must attend 504 plan meeting.	Parental consent is needed and a minimum amount of participants for meeting are stipulated.
Does not offer specific procedural safeguards.	Specific safeguards are included but are not limited to: the right to request an independent assessment at public expense and the student may "stay put" until a dispute is resolved.
Reports of noncompliance and the request for a hearing are made to the Office of Civil Rights.	Reports of noncompliance and request for due process are made to the State's Department of Education.

It is important to point out that just because your child has a diagnosis of Asperger's does not mean he will automatically qualify for any services. With more and more school districts cutting their special needs' budgets, some schools have made it near impossible to get your child an IEP or 504. The best thing is to educate yourself and know your rights.

School/Home Communication

A strong partnership between parents and teachers facilitates a successful education for all children. When you have a child with special needs, it is even more important that the doors of communication not only stay open but they swing both ways. The parent-teacher relationship is ongoing, mutual, respectful and, most importantly, child-centered. So how do we make it happen?

Email

The advancement of smart phones, which make it possible to check your messages anywhere at any time, makes email a very easy way for teachers to get in touch with parents these days. However, most teachers must wait until planning periods or afterschool to check and send email. For time-sensitive issues, this may not be the best form of communication. Keep in mind that sometimes emails can be misread or taken in a different tone or meaning than they were intended – something to remember when writing them. For this reason many school systems are discouraging their teachers from communicating with parents via email.

Phone calls

For complex issues, this is most likely the best communication option. Phone calls allow each party the opportunity to ask and receive answers to more complicated questions. However, they are not great for creating an ongoing dialogue exchange.

Student Planners

More and more schools are using student planners or agendas. The idea behind a planner is that it teaches the children organization skills and makes them responsible for their work assignments. Moms and dads can use the planner to communicate with the teacher on a daily basis as the teacher usually checks it. This is not an ideal method, though, if you don't want your child to see the message you are writing for the teacher.

Communication Log

This is my favorite form of communication and the one that I have found works best for Jay and his teachers. Many schools have ready-made logs, or you can simply make one up that will work for your child. Below is a sample of the one we use with Jay in middle school. What I love about this is that the teachers will write good things and not just bad. It not only acts as a way for them to stay in touch with me, but also, serves as an instant and very visual tool to Jay so that he knows immediately when he has done great or if he needs to work on something. It also informs me of unique circumstances, such as if there was a substitute, fire drill, assembly etc., which usually triggers some type of frustration, meltdown or anxiety behavior. I keep track of these and bring them with me to the IEP meetings.

Home – School Communication Log

Home-School Communication Log

Daily Log for

Date: 9-12 , 2012   Monday/ Tuesday /Wednesday /Thursday/ Friday

CLASS	BEHAVIOR
Math *Teacher initials* MS	☑ excellent ☑ average ☐ needs improvement Please comment on behavior (if *needs improvement* is selected, comments MUST be made):
Science *Teacher initials* LP	☑ excellent ☐ average ☐ needs improvement Please comment on behavior (if *needs improvement* is selected, comments MUST be made): waited patiently to be called on
U.S. History *Teacher initials* _____	☐ excellent ☐ average ☐ needs improvement Please comment on behavior (if *needs improvement* is selected, comments MUST be made):
Language Arts *Teacher initials*	☑ excellent ☐ average ☐ needs improvement Please comment on behavior (if *needs improvement* is selected, comments MUST be made): nice participation
Specials *(please indicate which class)* ☐ Art ☐Strings ☐PE ☐Health ☐Spectrum ☐Resource ☐Library ☐Keyboarding ☐SAMS *Teacher initials*	☑ excellent ☐ average ☐ needs improvement Please comment on behavior (if *needs improvement* is selected, comments MUST be made):
Specials *(please indicate which class)* ☐ Art ☐Strings ☐PE ☐Health ☒Spectrum ☐Resource ☐Library ☐Keyboarding ☐SAMS *Teacher initials*	☐ excellent ☒ average ☐ needs improvement Please comment on behavior (if *needs improvement* is selected, comments MUST be made): Some off-task conversation but completed an excellent draft of his mandala ... extremely creative

Other Events: ☐ Assembly ☐ Substitute Teacher for: _____ ☐ Other: _____

Transitioning to Middle School

The summer before Jay started middle school, I would wake up in cold sweats at night over the realization that my baby boy had graduated from elementary school and was about to enter the mean, scary hallways of middle school. Just when we finally had figured out the whole IEP process, we had to enter into the foreign world of secondary schools. Even though middle school means a new building, new teachers, new rules and a slew of new hormones, with a little extra preparation and a bit of parental advocacy, it doesn't have to be so daunting. While the following thoughts are mainly focused towards the elementary to middle school transition, many will work for the middle to high school transition as well.

Parent field trip time

Before your IEP transition meeting, do yourself a favor and tour the middle school that your child will be attending…without your child. Ask to see what an inclusion classroom looks like compared to a self-contained one. See how lockers are arranged and where bathrooms and counselors offices are in relation to them. In other words make a mental picture of how the school is laid out. You will be surprised at how just seeing the school and how it runs will alleviate much of your own anxiety.

Time to play with blocks

We aren't talking Legos either! One of the biggest differences between elementary school and middle/high school is that most middle and high schools use some sort of block scheduling such as 4 period days, A day/B day, A week/B week scheduling and so on. Some schools are also implementing a university model, which does not require students to be in the school building five days a week. The more familiar you get with the concept of A and B days or whatever your schools alternating block schedule is the easier it will be for you to help your child get the hang of it. Another helpful hint is to print out and laminate your child's schedule once they get it and post it in their locker as well in each class binder so they can refer to it should they forget what they have on what day.

If doesn't hurt to ask

Don't be afraid to ask questions and to ask for things that you feel will make your child's transition easier to be written into the IEP during your transitioning meeting. It is better to have too much than not enough. Little things like requesting to have a set of books to keep at home so that your child does not have to lug them back and forth, a locker on the end, near the bathrooms or a few extra minutes and/or help transitioning from class to class the first few weeks. These things can make a huge difference for your child.

Practice safe cracking

Go out and buy a combination lock and have your child practice, practice, practice using it all summer. The biggest fears that most kids have (both general ed and those with IEPs) are lockers and getting to class on time. Most kids can manage the number part, but it is the right-left-right thing that throws them off. If the lock is still a source of frustration for your child even after practicing for weeks, make sure to talk to the school about alternatives such as word combinations or a key lock.

Checking it once, then checking it twice

No, I'm not talking about whether your child is on the naughty or nice list. I'm talking about your child's schedule when you finally receive it in the mail. Make sure that all those

IEP services that you worked so hard to have included are there! If they are, great! Now you can take that schedule and your child to the school before opening day and walk through the schedule. If your child has something similar to an A day/B day schedule, I suggest going through the A day schedule one day and then returning a second day to walk through the B day schedule. The good thing about this is that some of the teachers are bound to be in the building, and although they will be busy and may not be able to meet with you, at least your child can put a face to a name.

Keep those worries fenced in

I'm talking about our worries, Mom and Dad. Remember what we talked about earlier in the book? Our kids feed off our own anxiety. What is that saying? Oh yeah, "Fake it until you believe it!" Keep telling yourself and your child that everything is going to be okay, and hopefully it will be!

Leading Your Aspie through Puberty

The day after Jay's 9th birthday, he came to me and said, "Okay, I am older now, so are you finally going to tell me where babies come from? The real story mom." I tried to laugh it off, but he was serious. I am no prude, but talking to my children about the "S" word was something I was just not prepared to do yet. Naively, I thought I would have at least another year or two before going there. I have never really talked to my other mommy friends about this. At what age are you supposed to have this dialog, and was my son emotionally ready for it?

All these thoughts and more were running through my head, as well as the thought, "Where is my husband?" Amazing how the guy is always on a business trip when these conversations pop up! I want my son to know that he can always talk to me about anything. I want him to not be afraid of his body. I also want him to hear things from me before he hears them from someone else. But what was I supposed to tell him? How much is too much? Not having the answers to these questions, I did what any other mother would have done – I winged it! In hind sight, this was one conversation for which I should have perhaps done a little prep work. But all in all, I think it went fairly well. (Being a writer, I quickly documented the whole talk, knowing that one day I would want to share this. Today is the day – lucky you!)

Here is how it went.

ME: "Jay, do you really want to know this? Are kids at school talking about it? What do you already know?"

JAY: "I know they don't really come from the stork. I know the baby grows in the mommy's belly. But how does it get there?"

ME: "Well, the daddy plants a seed in the mommy's belly." (Jay gives me a confused look, making me realize that I needed to explain quickly because my very literal son is imaging a tree growing in a mother's stomach.) "Okay, you know the difference between men and women, right? Men have a penis and women have a vagina. Well, the two are shaped very differently. God made it that way on purpose so that the two can fit together perfectly. (Another confused look, making me once again realize I needed a visual for him to understand. I shaped one hand into a circle and pointed my index finger on the other hand.)

JAY: "Oh I get it. Like a ring on a finger!"

ME: *"Exactly. And when the mommy and daddy fit together, the man's seed goes into the mommy. The seed meets up with an egg, which is already in the mommy, and that is how a baby is made. The baby will grow from that egg. It takes 9 months, and then the baby is ready to be born."*

(At this point my son had buried his head underneath his pillow.)

ME: *"I know it sounds kind of gross, right? What are you thinking? You okay?"*

JAY: *"I am thinking that if Gracie asks you this question, you should just keep with the stork version! Can we pretend we never had this discussion now?"*

ME: *(Trying not to laugh) "What conversation?"*

Puberty brings with it challenges for all children, but for our sensitive Aspies, there can be increased emotional changes, confusion, impulsive behaviors, depression, anxiety, moodiness and even anger with its good pal aggression right there with him. All those nasty hormones are enough to make a parent want to lock herself in the bathroom until it's all over. While the following tidbits of advice will not keep you from the occasional bathroom hideout, it may make this awkward transition a little easier for everyone.

The Talk

Puberty is an awkward time, not just for the kids, but for everyone. The body is starting to physically change, and with these changes may come some embarrassing questions. Your child needs someone to approach with these questions, and wouldn't you rather that be you than a peer who may not have the correct information, or as I once saw my son doing, consulting Google? That means you are going to have to suck it up and, whether your husband is home or not, have some uncomfortable conversations. If you wait for your child to come to you, it may never happen. So, be proactive and reach out to your child. Keep it age appropriate and remember: If you feel embarrassed talking about this, they'll feel embarrassed talking about it. Keep the innuendos and metaphors to a minimum because your kid may not get what the "Birds and Bees" have to do with sex.

Puberty Stinks

Literally! All those hormones and hair growing in different places add to that sweat – yeah, not a very pretty picture I just painted, is it? Our Aspies are not always good with change, and there is no greater change in one's life than puberty! That is why it is important to start establishing good hygiene habits way before puberty starts. If saying, "Hey, take a shower because no one wants to hang out with a stinky kid," doesn't work, use another more stealthy approach. Many Aspies just don't understand what the big deal is. If you have one of these kiddos, try this. Take a really smelly pair of their socks, and when they are not looking, put them inside their pillow case. When they lay down to go to sleep, they will most likely be disturbed by the smell and not be able to stand it. Explain to them that is what it is like to live with them. Then, while they are taking a shower, wash the socks!

Anger

Our Aspies are smart, and by the time they are going through puberty, they most likely have realized that they are a bit different than their peers. No matter how much we as parents try to make them see how wonderful diversity is, the bottom line is that teenagers want to fit in. Not wanting to stand out, they work very hard all day at school, trying their best to keep it together. That is a lot of work, so when they get home, they need a release. Like it or not, we parents are usually the ones on whom they take out their frustration. This is when you will need to remember the S.C.A.P.E. method, especially the stay calm part! It is important to not get emotionally involved, to breathe, and to let your child know that he can always come to you to talk. It is also important to establish acceptable boundaries. Physical violence is never an option, yelling obscenities at you will not be tolerated, etc. With every "NO, you can't do this," make sure you offer a "You CAN do this...." The angry meltdowns are not ideal, but it is certainly better than the alternative that some teenagers choose, not talking to you at all.

Socialization

Adolescence is a time when social demands become more complex, and it becomes increasingly important to be able to understand social cues. As stated above, fitting in is important and, because of this, kids with Asperger's are more susceptible to peer pressure and bullying. As parents, you can help by using social thinking and perspective taking techniques and games to help prepare them for possible scenarios they may be exposed to. There is a great game that I have played with Jay called "Should I or Shouldn't I" that covers all sorts of topics that really help with these issues. For more information on this game and for tons of other books and resources, check out the Social Thinking website at socialthinking.com.

The school years are about more than homework, report cards and proms. They are about teaching your child time management, organizational and daily living skills that will help make him more independent so that he can enter the next stage of life – adulthood.

Don't Freak Out

Chapter 8 Summary

- Work with your child's school, teachers and therapist to create an inclusive learning environment.
- A 504 <u>removes barriers</u> to foster equality.
- An IEP <u>adds services</u> to foster equality.
- The parent-teacher relationship is ongoing, mutual, respectful and most importantly child-centered.
- No matter how much we, as parents, try to make them see how wonderful diversity can be, teenagers just want to fit in.

Chapter 9

Siblings

Something happened a couple of years ago that really brought Grace and me closer together. It was a beautiful, cool evening, and a bunch of kids were outside playing in the common area of our neighborhood. I told my kids that they should go out and join them. Grace, who was 8 at the time, needed no prompting and quickly ran out. I was positive that Jay, who was 10, would chose to stay in, but he surprised me and said that he wanted to go out and play too.

The kids were already in the middle of a game of tag, and Grace easily incorporated herself into the action. Jay cautiously approached the group. I beamed with pride when I heard him ask the kids, "Can I play too?" To other parents, this may not seem like a big deal, but as you know, to an autism mom or dad, those words are pure gold!

The kids shrugged and said, "Sure," and then tried to tell him what team he was on. Jay, not knowing the rules, got confused and started to tell the other children how they should be playing. As you can imagine, this did not go over well. The other children started to protest. Jay got upset and ran from the scene, plopped his crying self onto the sidewalk and did his best to try to pull himself together. He was halfway through a yoga pose, breathing heavily in and out, when I heard one of the other kids say to Grace, "What is the matter with him?" I looked to Grace to see what she was going to do. Would she try to explain to the kids what the problem was? "My brother has Asperger's. He gets overwhelmed sometimes. My mom is with him, so he'll be okay. But thanks for asking about him!" But Grace did not say that. Grace did not come over to see if he was indeed okay. She dismissed him. Perhaps it was a typical 8-year-old sibling reaction. Okay, I know it was a typical 8-year-old sibling reaction, but we are not the typical family.

I admit that my heart broke a little.

After making sure Jay was okay, I called Grace over to tell her I was a little disappointed. She argued with me, saying that Jay was not following the rules, not playing fair and all the other typical responses that siblings say when they are trying to get out of trouble.

I admit that my heart broke even more.

Once inside the house, I tried again to talk to her. She painfully tried to explain to me that I did not understand how hard it was to be Jay's sister. Then it happened. Somehow the words just poured out. I admitted to my child something that I had never admitted out loud! I pulled her onto my lap, and said,

"I know it's hard. I get it, really, I do because it is hard for me too. I say all the time that I want everyone to accept Jay for the way he is, but some days, some days, I can't help but think it would be so much easier if he was just a bit more like everyone else."

I actually gasped after I finished saying it. I was shocked to have heard the words spoken aloud. Grace just sat there unsure of what of what she should say, so I continued on.

"But as hard as it for us, think how hard it must be for Jay."

We talked about how to us he is just JAY, but to others he may seem...different. We talked about how people treat others who are different from them. We talked about how important it is for us to help Jay find his place in the world, to make him feel welcomed, and encourage him to be a part of it.

And of course we talked about Grace. How special she is. How I know she has a heart as big as Texas and why it makes me sad when she does not let others see it! How what she says or, in this case, what she did not say makes a huge difference. We talked about how even though she is the younger sibling, she needs to keep an eye on Jay because that is what family does. We look out for one another.

Then Grace excused herself and quietly walked downstairs to where Jay was watching TV, oblivious to the emotional scene taking place just a floor above him. She walked over to her brother and told him she needed a hug. Jay stopped watching TV. He looked at his sister's red eyes and tear-stained cheeks, hugged her and asked, "Are you okay Grace?" To which she replied, "I am now!"

I admit it...my heart melted!

Fairness

While the story above is touching and has a happy ending, it also produced much guilt for me. The constant feeling that I am not there for both of my children is never ending. If you have more than one child, I am sure you can relate. I love both my kids equally. That said, there is no way that I can possibly devote an equal amount of time and attention to them both. At one time or another, one child's needs are going to take precedence over the others, and yes, the reality is that often that someone getting more of Mommy's attention is Jay.

Exactly how the neuro-typical children in a household respond to having a sibling with autism depends on the ages of the kids, their maturity and the overall family dynamic. If you are feeling guilty, guess what, they will think there is something to feel guilty about. That may cause even more jealousy and resentment. So, what do you do to not make that happen?

It took me a while to realize this, but finally it hit home. I'm not sure where the saying came from, but once I heard it, I immediately printed it out, and the paper is prominently displayed on our refrigerator for all to see.

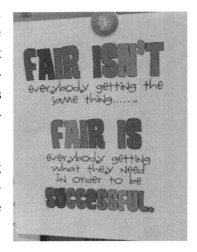

"Fairness isn't everyone getting the same thing...Fairness is everybody getting what they need to be successful."

That includes Mom and Dad's attention. I am not sure who that saying helps more, me or Grace, but nonetheless, seeing it on the fridge every time I go in there, (which some days is a lot) is good for us both. Do I still get, "It's not fair," every now and again? Yup, but even parents of non-special needs children get that!

Now that we got that out of the way and removed all the guilt, let's talk about siblings and what you as the parent can do to help foster a healthy relationship among your children.

Sources of Sibling Stress

While much research confirms that the majority of brothers and sisters of children with autism cope well with their experiences, it does not mean that they do not encounter special challenges. There are potential sources of stress for these siblings.

Not all siblings will experience these issues, but you should be aware of a few of the following possible situations:

- Not really understanding what Autism/Asperger's is.
- Jealousy over the amount of parental time and attention received by the sibling.
- Frustration over not having a typical sibling relationship.
- Embarrassment about certain behaviors or perhaps lack of action (especially when peers are around).
- Being the target of their sibling's aggressive behaviors.
- Concern over parent's feelings.
- Future concerns about what will happen to their sibling.
- A need to be extra perfect to make up for their sibling's deficits and challenges.

Explaining Asperger's to Your Other Children

Here is the thing: as a parent, you get a chance to warm up to the idea of Asperger's. You start to see differences, you do your research, you get a diagnosis and then you deal with it. The word Asperger's or Autism has meaning, you know what it stands for, and you understand the challenges that come along with that title. For the sibling, it is just a word. The brother or sister is just a brother or sister. In a way, it is a beautiful thing. Sure, they might be frustrated by their sibling, but it is the actual person, not a diagnosis that upsets them. (Think about it.)

Basically, that means you will need to try to explain to your child what the "word" means. Keep the conversation age appropriate and positive. Yes, it is important to share with your Neurotypical child the challenges their brother and sister have, but it is even more important to point out all the benefits. There are some great books you could read together as well as websites and other resources (check out the resource section in this chapter and at the end of the book as a starting point) that may be helpful in getting the conversation started.

Be prepared for questions, and be honest if you don't know the answers. Just because a young child has the word Asperger's in his vocabulary, doesn't mean he really understands. With that in mind, you will need to keep having conversations with your children periodically to make sure they get what it means.

NOTE: Whenever possible, the Asperger's diagnosis should be disclosed to the child with Asperger's FIRST, before it is explained to siblings.

Helping your children develop relationships

Most siblings have a mixture of emotions towards their brothers or sisters. Feelings of love and affection one minute can turn to anger and frustration the next, but don't all children feel that? If you are fortunate to have a sibling, think back to when you were growing up and your relationship with your siblings. Most likely, your sibling was the source of your torment, your partner in crime, your playmate and ally all rolled up into one. Isn't this what you want for your children too?

Most Aspies benefit greatly from their neurotypical sibling. Siblings make up their very own social group, and it is a safe place to learn about the way the world works and how to behave appropriately. For kids who have a hard time making friends, their siblings may be their only peer interaction. So, how do you as a parent help your children develop a great relationship (or any relationship, for that matter)?

First, it is important to remember that sibling rivalry is not only normal, it is important. As long as things are not turning physical or getting too out of hand, try to sit back and let your kids work things out on their own. It is a great way for both kids to practice problem solving skills and compromise. Whenever possible, don't try to automatically rescue your children by implementing the boss parenting style. Instead, act as the consultant and offer advice that helps them see the problems in a different way. By doing this, neither child feels as if you are taking the other's side, which is an important thing to establish, especially with kids who already are feeling left out or as if they don't matter as much as the special need's child does.

Kids with Asperger's can be highly over-focused or have certain obsessions. I'm sure that you know what I mean by this. Just think about how annoyed you sometimes feel when your son goes on and on about a super villain while you are trying to talk on the phone. Now, imagine how your non-Aspie child may feel? It is hard to develop a relationship with someone who is only interested in certain things and does not give you a chance to express your thoughts and opinions or have a turn in a conversation. In our house we use the concept of a traffic light to help with this.

Red Light = Stop

Yellow Light = Proceed with Caution

Green Light = Go

When Jay gets overly excited about something and is just talking on and on and not even noticing that no one is really listening any more, we say, "Red Light!" My rule-following Aspie knows that red light means stop, so even though he does not want to, he stops talking. Grace now uses this with Jay as well. "Jay, Red Light. I know you are super excited about that Batman show and all, but I really need to finish my homework now, so perhaps you can tell me about it at dinner?" Jay happily stops, but you better believe he will pick up exactly where he left off at dinner.

This is also a great tool to use when we are in public and Jay is doing something that could be considered inappropriate or strange to others. When we say "red light," it stops him in his tracks. It gives him a second to review the situation in a new perspective and see how it might be perceived to others and then figure out on his own a different choice that he could make. Even if he doesn't agree, he respects the other person enough to stop. There is no overly dramatic scene about how Jay is bothering Grace or how embarrassing he is being, etc. The outsider may think the term Red Light is strange, but usually it goes unnoticed.

Here's an example of how it can be used in public: We are at a restaurant. Jay is very hungry, and he sees other people getting their food while we are still waiting for ours. He starts to stand up to yell to the waitress across the room. Before he can do it, we say Red Light! Jay stops, sits back down and processes what just happened. When the waitress comes closer, he says calmly and politely, "Excuse me, but will our food be coming out soon?" He is still getting to express his concern, to ask his question, but is now doing it in a different way. He is happy because he gets an answer. We are happy because he made a more appropriate choice to go about receiving an answer. All because of a two word prompt.

Since we started this Traffic Light idea, the kids get along much better as they both feel as if they are being heard and given a chance to speak. Jay will even use it on us. "Mom, Red Light. You are talking too fast, and it is hurting my head." It is much easier to get along with anyone when you feel the other person respects you. In our family, the use of the Traffic Light is a way for people to express what they need to in a respectful way. In other words, the Red Light is meaning, "I respect that this is important to you, but you need to respect me and stop right now." I must warn you, though, it doesn't work as well on husbands, not that I have tried or anything.

Helping the Non-Aspie Child Feel Special

Yes, I wrote about how fair does not mean that everyone receives the same thing. That said, your child is going to feel the way your child feels. Most likely, those feelings of being left out, not special, less important.

That is why it is important that you carve out some special time just for your non-Aspie. I know, I know, there is no time, there is no money! It doesn't have to be a whole day that depletes your saving's account. It could be making the non-Aspie's favorite meal for dinner, even though that means you will have to make your Aspie something else because you know there is no way in hell he is going to eat lasagna because the stuff is all mixed together! It could mean a sleepover in the non-Aspie's bedroom, where you stay up talking when everyone else is asleep. It could mean a girls' day out to get your nails done and have lunch. What does your child like? More importantly, what does your child need?

Gracie bakes with me. I have to admit that the OCD in me doesn't like the mess she makes, and it takes everything I have to not grab the bowl from her and mix the batter the "right" way. But, I fight those urges. It really isn't about the product we end up with anyway; although, we do make some killer chocolate chip cookies together. It is about the connection we have when we are standing side-by-side, doing something together. We laugh, sometimes we cry, but mostly we laugh. No matter how busy she knows I am, no matter how often she may feel that she gets the short end of stick, for that half an hour, it is just her and me, and she feels great. And you know what? I feel great too.

Sibling Groups and Resources

Even if you are making special time for your non-Aspie, she still may feel stressed. Hey, you think you are the only one with that corner of the market? Seeking out a professional for siblings to talk with may be something worth investigating. It doesn't have to be a psychiatrist or a therapist. I approached the school counselor. I met with her and told her how anxious Gracie was. I told her how I knew there must be other kids in school who had siblings with special needs and how it would be great if Grace could somehow connect with them. So the wonderful counselor put together a weekly lunch bunch group of siblings of special needs kids. It made a huge difference for Grace. Suddenly, she didn't feel so alone, so guilty about being upset or frustrated. There were other kids like her who got it. I don't think I could give my girl a better gift than that!

There are many groups that exist to support the entire family, including siblings. To locate a sibling support group in your area, contact the National Autism Society of America at www.autism-society.org.

One main program that many siblings find to be not only helpful but also fun is Sibshop. "Sibshops acknowledge that being the brother or sister of a person with special needs is for

some a good thing, others a not-so-good thing, and for many, somewhere in-between. They reflect a belief that brothers and sisters have much to offer one another — if they are given a chance." The Sibshop curriculum is used throughout the United States, Canada, England, Ireland, Iceland, Japan, New Zealand, Guatemala, Turkey and Argentina:
www.siblingsupport.org/sibshops/find-a-sibshop.

SibTeen is a place on the internet just for teens. SibTeen is now available both as a Yahoo group and a Facebook group:

www.siblingsupport.org/connect/sibteen-facebook-group-and-yahoogroup.

Books
The following books deal with disclosure for children with Asperger's, their siblings and extended family members:

Can I Tell You About Asperger Syndrome?: A Guide for Friends and Family - by Jude Welton

All Cats Have Asperger Syndrome - by Kathy Hoopman

Brotherly Feelings: Me, My Emotions, and My Brother with Asperger's Syndrome -by Sam Frender and Robin Schiffmiller

The following books are children's fiction stories that include a character with Asperger's:

Lisa and the Lacemaker: An Asperger Adventure -by Kathy Hoopmann

Wishing On the Midnight Star: My Asperger Brother - by Nancy Ogaz

The Reinvention of Edison Thomas - by Jacqueline Houtman

Blue Bottle Mystery: An Asperger Adventure - by Kathy Hoopmann

 *Don't Freak Out*

Chapter Nine Summary

- Fairness doesn't mean that everyone receives the same thing. Fairness means that everybody receives what they need to be successful.
- The majority of brothers and sisters of children with autism cope well with their experiences.
- Most siblings have a mixture of emotions towards their brother or sister. They may feel love and affection one minute, anger and frustration the next.
- Sibling rivalry is not only normal, it is important.
- It is important that you carve out some special time just for your non-Aspie.
- Having your non-Aspie talk to a professional or joining a sibling support group can be helpful for your child.

Chapter 10

Valuable Insights from Adult Aspies

I am not proud to admit this, but if you would have asked me 20 years ago to describe autism, I would have mentioned kids sitting, rocking in a corner and flapping their hands or Rain Man. How naïve I was, how close-minded, and uneducated. The only image I had of Autism at that time was the one that was portrayed in the media. The "me" of twenty years ago, carefree in her twenties, not married and childfree, knew nothing about high-functioning autism or Asperger's, and the word "spectrum" brought images of colors on a rainbow. Back then I had certain ideas about how things were supposed to be, what normal was and how "normal" should look. It was easy to accept the image of the way things were portrayed in the movies and on TV. Why wouldn't I?

So here I am, twenty years later, certainly more weathered but I would like to think wiser too. The way I view the world now has less to do with my maturity and more to do with my son. Yup, this brilliant, diverse young person has exposed me to so much wonder and forced me to question what the rest of the world sees and accepts. How beautiful is that?

But here is the thing: It took me a while to get here, this place I am now. Sure, I have always accepted my son and his diagnosis. But for a while I thought of Asperger's as something that happens instead of something that is. The two are very different. Asperger's did not just happen; it is part of what makes my boy, my boy. But now I know it is even more than that.

My aha moment happened while reading an article about mind blindness and how this is supposed to be a character trait of most people with Asperger's. Mind blindness is defined as the incapacity to comprehend the state of mind of others, their wants, beliefs, feelings and intentions. It is the inability to understand what others may be thinking or wishing.

Suddenly, it hit me like a ton of bricks. We, as a society, are so quick to judge, to label our Aspies as the ones who are mind blind when in reality, perhaps we are. I could not tell you what my boy is thinking, feeling, all his wants, beliefs and intentions, and I am so-called neurotypical. Never mind being typical, I am his mother for goodness sake. He is one of two people in this entire universe who knows what my heart sounds like from the inside, and yet, do I really know him? I think I know him, what he needs wants and believes based on my own thoughts, wants and beliefs. What makes my way correct and his way incorrect? Perhaps he is the one who is seeing, and I am the one who is mind blind.

This revaluation brought a whole new perspective. I realized that no matter how good my intentions are, no matter how hard I try, I will never truly understand what it is like for my boy because I do not have Asperger's. Thankfully, my boy Jay is getting older and is finding ways – or should I say I am finding ways – to understand what he has already been showing me, what it is he needs and wants to help him reach his full potential.

That said, there are still many days that I am left scratching my head, wondering what I can do, or should have done, to help. This is why I think it is so important that we parents connect to adults who actually have Asperger's. (And that our children connect with other Aspies too!) That we listen to the Aspie grownups who understand, and are now able to express what they are feeling in a way that allows us to finally get what it is our children are trying to tell us. This is why this chapter, in my opinion, is perhaps the most important one in this book.

This chapter gives voice to where the voice belongs. It is a chance for parents to hear firsthand from people who have been where our kids are now. It is also a chance for these incredibly insightful writers to put misconceptions and myths to rest. Their stories offer us a glimpse into what it is that our children may be feeling but cannot yet express.

Read what these folks have written. Words matter. What we say to our children matters. What our children hear matters even more. There is a reason why the title of this chapter is valuable insights. I have no doubt that the way you view your child, the way you view yourself, the way you view this beautiful world in which we live will change after reading the following.

Kate Goldfield

aspiefrommaine.blogspot.com

Have you ever wondered what it is like to be 20-something with Asperger's? Kate Goldfield's blog, *Aspie from Maine*, explores that question. Her blog is not just limited to an audience of people in their 20s; it is for anyone who has ever wanted to know anything about autism. It delves into the nature and experiences of autism and examines it from as many angles as possible. Kate's goal is to start conversations between people with Asperger's or autism, parents of kids with autism spectrum disorders and anyone who just wants to know more. The following post by Kate first appeared on her blog back in December of 2012. The first time I read it, I wept because the words she chose to use touched me so much.

When I decided to write this chapter, I knew right away that I wanted to include this piece, and Kate was kind enough to allow me to do so. Make sure to check out Kate's blog and also her book *Common Scents: Adventures with Autism and Chemical Sensitivity,* the story of a young woman's search for physical and emotional safety as she journeys through the Cascade Mountains, small coastal towns along the Oregon coast and out-of the-way towns in upstate New York. Along the way, she experiences things she would never have dreamed possible had she stayed in her Maine hometown and begins to learn the power of human connection. For more information or to purchase her book, visit http://kategoldfield.webs.com.

Use Your Words

by Kate Goldfield

"Use your words" is a statement often used with small kids who are pushing and shoving or otherwise behaving in what is considered an unreasonable manner. It is a reminder to use language rather than behavior. Behavior clearly is communication, but not always the most useful form of it.

This post, however, is about a different form of using your words. It is about using words to define yourself. It is about the words others use to define you - or don't.

Words are powerful. Words have the ability to shape lives. Your whole idea of how the world works, your whole idea of who you are, and your role in the world. All defined by words - or feelings that originated in words.

What do you remember about the way you were described as a child? What is your first memory of yourself? I was described as smart - although I always knew there was something wrong or different about me. There were no words for that, though. Asperger's was not a diagnosis I would get for another dozen years or so. I was told that my intelligence would come in handy when I was older. I have one memory of a summer camp of some sort. Sitting on a gym mat. A teenage counselor telling me I seemed much older than the other campers, more mature. All good things, she assured me.

But how? How could these be good things? I was 10 (and 8, and 12, and 14, and you get the idea). I wanted to know why I wasn't like the other kids my age. I wanted to fit in. I wanted to be able to talk to them. I wanted to be, just once, not so "separate." And I would have traded all the smartness in the world for it.

Sometimes I was "sweet." Sweet is such a non-specific word. I grew to hate it. Wasn't there anything else good about me? So far I knew that I was smart and I was sweet. Not exactly the recipe for success in my book.

This was countered by far, far too many messages from my peers about being different, awkward, weird, and "other." Messages about being socially incompetent, even about being selfish or deeply flawed in some way. These messages were not usually specific, but they were coming from everywhere, every corner of my existence, so they must be true. They didn't hold a candle to "smart" or "sweet."

People believe that they are who they are unless given good reason to believe otherwise. I think there is a lack of positive reinforcement in our culture. Good traits are rarely highlighted. People rarely have the opportunity to change their mind about themselves for the better, unless they meet someone willing to show them, and to be persistent about it.

I finally had the opportunity, recently, at 28, to begin to have cause to redefine my 20-year-old perception of myself. I joined a meet-up group where the members seemed welcoming and to genuinely like me. Yes, this comes as a surprise. I imagine it will for quite some time, but it's a start.

I met a longtime blogging friend in real life who, after the meeting, devoted a whole blog to that meeting. Make sure to visit Jess's blog at *Diary of a Mom*. Her blog nearly brought me to tears. She used her words. Thank you, Jess, for using your words.

The concrete things that I knew about Kate are that she has Asperger's, and also that she has some pretty serious sensitivity to fragrances and chemicals that can make life particularly challenging. So that's what I knew. But please believe me when I tell you this — those are NOT the things that you notice when you meet Kate. Instead, what you see — what you can't possibly miss — is her energy. ~ Jess from Diary of a Mom

www.adiaryofamom.wordpress.com/2012/12/04/kate

The silent, unanswered questions about what I could possibly have to offer someone – the perception of myself as a burden – began to be erased, as if with a Magic Marker, with Jess's words. Oh, sweet words, a gift to me to begin to redefine myself.

A friend tells me I bring out the kid in him and make him feel carefree. Another friend, who I more recently met, tells me that I would make a good therapist because my experiences bring about a sense of empathy and openness to other's experiences that she finds very attractive.

Words, words. They are simply words, but they have the power to change a life. Mine. Yours. Everyone's. We need to be honest with each other, not just about what our friends and loved ones have to work on, but what we love about them, and why. We need to use our words. We need to be a community.

"You are at a point where trust in life and your spirit, higher self or soul is paramount or even trust in the goodness of the universe. You are at a place in your life where you are pregnant with potential which is filled with your greatest wishes and your greatest

fears; it is up to you which ones you will give power to."

The above is a quote from a recent meet-up I attended. I can't think of anything more accurate for where I am in my life than those words. Which will I choose? Will I have the strength and resources I need to choose my dreams over my fears?

It feels as though I've spent my life living as a 'one-woman island,' perhaps due to my Asperger's. Or perhaps due to the confluence of many different forces, no one's "fault" but present nonetheless.

So my single, number one goal now is to find community and build social connections. Because only with that can I find the strength, courage and resilience to choose my dreams over my fears. I can't be an island anymore. I'm not saying this as it's a done deal. I don't know how it will go. But I've made a good start. And I know that words, different words, a different community, a different environment and different experiences will hopefully produce a different person. Or at least the same person who thinks quite differently about herself - and therefore will become a different, and better, person.

You spend the first thirty or so years of your life learning about yourself and the world around you.

Then, depending on your life experiences, you can spend the rest of your life trying to un-learn these things.

Nicholas T. Falls

www.facebook.com/Hipster.Autistic.Dad

When I decided to write this chapter I contacted many of the people I know in the Autism community and asked if they would like to contribute. The response I got back from Mr.

Falls... well, let's just say he definitely put me in my place. Here is what he wrote back.

"I would be willing to write a short bit on some specific topic. I also think you will find this to be the case for most autistics. Good responses only come from good questions. Otherwise we tend to just disengage when the questions or requests are too vague for our way of thinking."

Yup, here I was asking him to contribute to write but was quite vague in the way I approached him. I responded by asking him to write about exactly that, how we parents tend to be rather vague with our kids. What he sent me back was pure gold, and I know that it will be of benefit to many of you.

Before I get to his piece on Regular Communication, let me tell you a bit about Nicholas T. Falls. Nicholas, who is also known as Hipster Autistic Dad on Facebook, is from Missouri. Hipster Sr. was only diagnosed as an Aspie after his son, Hipster Jr. received his official diagnosis. Together, the Hipsters are looking for ways to help others enjoy the sort of life that they do, one that is not perfect but is enjoyable more often than not. Hipster Sr. has a book written in his head and is just waiting for the right time and person to help him get it onto paper. I, for one, cannot wait for that to happen. It will no doubt be a best-seller because, as the Hipster says, *"I'm not aiming at you, but I'm not trying to miss..."*

Regular Communication
by Nicholas T. Falls

A common concern with many parents is the feeling they have that the child isn't willing to share with them what's going on in their life. This is usually anything but true assuming the child hasn't already given up being able to share with their parents. They are often more than willing and even desire to share, but may not know how or feel safe to do so.

First of all do not try to press them for information when they are already stressed or upset. If communication is difficult and you're already stressed having someone bombard you with questions is torture. Parents often bemoan the lack of what they see as regular communication when the problem is usually the way the parents engage their child. They ask poor/vague questions and often respond poorly or harshly to honest responses. Typical NT questions are too vague for an autistic child to reply to. "How was your day?" is not going to get you very far. What's going to help is listening to what they do mention, and then asking specific questions about what they have chosen to share.

So if you want better regular communication, I suggest having a regular series of specific questions that you go through. This sort of routine helps because it can be something that is consistent and not just something where the only time the child thinks you care about what's going on is when they are in trouble or in conflict. If the child thinks that's all you really care about they are going to be far less likely to share with you. Good questions will be specific:

"What did you eat for lunch today?"
"Who did you sit with?"
"What did you do in science today?"
"What did you do during recess today?"

I know that these will seem too simple and yet if you try them you might find they do work. The way these help is by opening the door to communication. Once they respond to a factual question they will often volunteer something more. Then you can ask questions that lead them to talk about things in a deeper manner. After they share something good questions can help them understand their own feelings better and give you better insight into their life. Questions to dig deeper look like:

"How did you feel about that?"

"What would you have liked to have happen?"
"Why do you think they did that?"

The responses to those are more likely to get you the information about how they feel. It is absolutely essential that you learn to listen to understand not to judge. When they share why they think someone did something be careful not to immediately make their thoughts and feelings wrong, validate those feelings before addressing the possible flaws in their logic. One of my favorite things to do when things don't make sense at work or in life in general is to ask someone, "You know why they do it this way don't you?" of course they respond "No." I reply, "Because they're a bunch of assholes, I don't know who "they" are, but I'm sure they do."... nod...

If they say they think their teacher did something because their teacher hates them, they are sharing their feelings about that relationship. If you immediately say "That's not true" you will probably find them less willing to share their feelings in the future. So make sure that you are a safe person to share with if you want them to share. If sharing honest feelings results in disappointment on the part of the parent that too is discouraging and results in less communication.

So for better communication remember the three S's.
Specific, Simply, and Safe

Questions should be specific and simply, and the environment (parental response) safe.

Scott Lentine

Scott Lentine is an amazingly talented 25-year-old poet with high-functioning autism from Billerica, Massachusetts. Scott, who was completely non-verbal until the age of 5, graduated magna cum laude from Merrimack College with a Bachelor's Degree in Religious Studies and a minor in Biology. He currently works as a public policy intern at The Arc of

Massachusetts in Waltham and is dedicated to improving resources in his state for people with developmental disabilities. His hobbies include poetry, going to the beach, reading, watching movies and documentaries, meeting new people and playing with dogs. His poems about autism have been recognized by people such as Seth Mnookin, John Sebastian, Tom Rush and many autism advocates including John Elder Robison, Susan Senator and Stephen Shore. I am so privileged to be able to include a few of his pieces in this book.

Just a Normal Day
by Scott Lentine

Never knowing what to say
Never knowing what to do
Always looking for clues
Just a normal day

Feeling unsure
Totally perplexed with everyday life
Always on edge never certain
I wish I could lift this curtain
Needing to constantly satisfy my need for information
Always online searching for new revelations
Going from site to site
Obtaining new insights every night

Trying to connect with people my age
Attempting to reveal my unique vision
But ending up alone and unengaged
Feeling like my life needs a total revision
Just a normal day

Can't You See
by Scott Lentine

Can't you see
I just want to have a friend
Can't you see
I need the same connections in the end

Can't you see
I want a good job
Can't you see
I need to have stability and dependence and part of the general
mob
Can't you see
I want to be independent on my own
Can't you see
I want to be able to have my own home

Can't you see
I want the same things as everyone else
Can't you see
I want to be appreciated for myself

The Ode to the Autistic Man
by Scott Lentine

Try to understand the challenges that I face
I would like to be accepted as a human in all places
Where I will end up in life I don't know
But I hope to be successful wherever I go
I would like to expand my social skills in life
Making new friends would be very nice

Stand proud for the autistic man
For he will find a new fan
I hope to overcome the odds I face today
Increased acceptance will lead me to a brighter day

By the age of 20, I will have made tremendous strides

I know in the future, life will continue to be an interesting ride
I have made new friends by the year
I will be given tremendous respect by my family and peers
I hope to get noted for bringing the issue of autism to the common man
So that autistic people can be accepted in this great land

Stand proud for the autistic man
For he will find a new fan
I hope to overcome the odds I face today
Increased acceptance will lead me to a brighter day

Kansas Moskwik

Kansas is a 21-year-old Aspie who runs a video blog on autism on her YouTube channel: kansas moskwik.

Her passion in life is helping others like herself as well as parents of children with Asperger's. What I love about Kansas is how honest she is. She talks so freely and is heartfelt about her relationship with her fiancé. It warms my soul to see how in love they both are. Don't take my word for it. Read for yourself.

Asperger's and Love
by Kansas Moskwik

There are many myths surrounding Autism and Asperger's, and they are not true for most of us. One of the biggest ones is that we cannot truly feel and show love for others. Many people believe that we will have hard times finding true love and keeping it. This is not true; we are loving people. It's hard to find the one no matter what. You don't have to have autism to have a hard time finding that one special person.

In August of 2012 I met a man named Andrew who was also has Asperger's. We hit it off right away and I knew he was the one for me. Our love for Star Wars and comic books brought us together. I am not the type of girl to flirt or make the first move, but with him I did, and I am glad I did. We met at a trade school in Vermont, he was a business student and me, well put it this way I stayed for love and didn't care too much for the program but I still tried my best.

Andrew and I were close right off the bat and we were never apart. Within the first month of dating we knew everything about each other. I also knew I loved him, but I worried he didn't feel the same way. Two months into our relationship we took a long walk up a large hill that overlooked our school's campus. It was a beautiful fall day. We sat together talking about our lives and our struggles with autism. I looked at him and I told him that I needed to tell him something. There was a long silence as he waited for me to speak. Finally I looked at him and said that I loved him. For the first time he looked me in the eye's with his icy blue eyes, and all he said was "I know."

For those of you who do not know, that is what Han Solo told Princess Leia when she told him that she loved him for the first time. And as I have mentioned before Andrew and I were brought together through our love for Star Wars. After that we were even closer. About a few weeks later he was over at my house, we took a long walk to a local cemetery, something that I personally enjoy to visit. That is when we first talked about marriage, we are unofficially engaged. Now we are officially, and are planning a large nerd themed wedding.

People have told us that we will never make it because of our autism that we cannot show each other how we truly feel. Nor can we hold a relationship that is both physical and emotional. We have proved all those people wrong. Our love is strong and everlasting. We are each other's shields in the battle we fight against our struggles and the candle in the dark. He is my world and I am his. He changed my life as I changed his. I truly believe that nothing will stop us and we will keep proving people wrong.

It has now been one year since we got together. It has been the happiest of my life. For the first time in my life I am truly and honestly happy. He made my life complete and I think I did the same for him. Andrew is the best thing that happened to me. And I hope our story can give other people with autism hope that one day they will find that one person as they live their life and overcome the struggles that we go through.

Charlie Henbury

Charlie is a young man with a bright future ahead of him. At 18 he considers himself to be quite the actor, filmmaker, DJ and, of course, writer. I was introduced to Charlie online, and when I saw his "about me" page with the following quote, "Autism is not a disability; it's a hidden gem ability," I knew I wanted to include him and hear more about what he had to say.

I admit that I was a bit vague (hey, it was before I learned my lesson from Nicholas) when I asked him to submit anything he wanted. But Charlie came through. He sent back this short poem that, well, I could easily see my boy writing. The words are few, but the meaning is deep. This is what Charlie's Autism looks like.

Conscientious about the outside world into the unknown. Forming sweet melody majestic friendships, or even relationships Myself have Obsessions with objects, ideas or desire that's my Autism Including Abnormal use of pitch, intonation, rhythm or stress.

Ms. A.J. Mahari

http://aspergeradults.ca
http://ajmahari.ca

A.J. Mahari is a professional writer and a life coach and was diagnosed with Asperger's Syndrome in adulthood. She believes her Asperger's is a different ability, not a disability. She has taught herself how to map out Aspie social/communication challenges using her narrow focus of interest to continue to extend her own limits and to create her own successful business.

I am not sure how I fell upon A.J.'s website, but I am so glad I did. I spent a good couple of hours there, just reading all her articles. It was the piece below that resonated with me. I immediately contacted A.J., told her about this project and begged to have her allow me to use this piece. In an effort to reach more parents, she eagerly agreed.

Do Aspies Have Empathy For Others?
by A.J. Mahari

Almost every definition I've ever read about Asperger's Syndrome lists among the traits and/or characteristics attributed to those with it as not being able to feel empathy for others – as not having empathy for others. I have Asperger's Syndrome. I have tremendous capacity for empathy for others. I have continued to increase my ability to express that empathy. Do Aspies really lack empathy or is it felt, experienced, and expressed differently? Perhaps in ways that neurotypicals (NT's) do not recognize as empathy or do not experience as being the way they expect to be given empathy.

As I've likely written about in other contexts related to Asperger's Syndrome, it seems reasonable to say that there are many differences in those who have Asperger's Syndrome (AS). Men and women seem to have differing ability and context as well as understanding when it comes to something like empathy and compassion as well. (Attwood) There is still a difference not only in the way boys and girls are socialized, what those social norms contain, but also in what society expects from boys versus girls. Attwood, in his book, "The Complete Guide To Asperger's Syndrome" talks about this and concludes that females find ways to learn to express and to care-giver in ways that perhaps many Aspie males don't.

In my own experience with empathy, as an adult with AS, I know that I feel tremendous empathy for others. That can be someone I am talking to, sitting in a room with, or someone I see on the evening news who has suffered a tragic loss. There is also a very profound sense of connectedness to humanity in its macrocosm that means I experience a lot of empathy and compassion for a lot of world events and things that I see on the news and so forth that aren't a part of my own life.

A lot of this empathy that I have and feel that is palpable within me there isn't maybe as much expression of it at times. It depends if I am coaching with someone, or writing. If I am just in my own world, doing my own thing, in the splendor and wonder of my narrow focuses of interest (which are in themselves paradoxically vast) then there is much more that I feel that others can't know – that isn't measurable.

The way that Asperger's Syndrome is defined, like many other pervasive developmental disorders, or even mental illnesses pathologies and categorizes differences in what are highly divisive and negative ways. There is little if any consideration given to the different ability of many with Asperger's in and through which things are felt, experienced, processed, and expressed differently. Not being the same as the feelings, experiences, processing, and expression of neurotypicals (NT's) the presumed NT's who set out the defining criteria of Asperger's Syndrome fail to give consideration to different ability. What is different about those with AS in the minds of those defining it and those who continue to forward that narrow definition of it, despite endless individual manifestations and expressions of AS from all the people who have it, is that there is a tremendous lack of tolerance for difference.

It's as if there is some segment of society, "professionals" (?) that are charged with defining the ever-elusive "normal". It's flawed logic to begin with. It leaves no room for each to march to the beat of his or her own drummer, to be introverted versus extroverted without scrutiny and/or without penalty of judgment and being pathologized.

I don't happen to think there is anything particularly horribly wrong with my brain as someone with Asperger's Syndrome. Again, the differences between Aspie brains and NT brains see the NT's pathologize the Aspie brains as "dysfunctional". Why not just different? For all that people with Asperger's have contributed to this world through the unique genius that is a bonus to our differences, geez, I don't see that being categorized as negatively as the ways in which we "don't get NT social". Who needs it? I mean I straddle that line. I have pushed myself way far to "get it". However, "getting it" to some extent, and being able to connect socially, feel and express empathy and receive it doesn't mean that I want or need to be in that "space" that often. I just don't. I do find myself in that space in terms of the work I do, writing I do, and knowing what others need from me at times. The rest of the time, time I can have for me, in my splendid Aspie world, is time cherished. That is not a statement about egocentrism or being unaware. Again, it's difference.

The egocentrism of my Asperger's is something that I am now very aware of. There are ways around it. Do they feel natural? No. Will they ever? I doubt it. Does it matter to me – not any more.

There are also many feelings, such as love, empathy, compassion, and so forth that are compromised to varying degrees with individuals with Asperger's Syndrome. This does mean they can't continue to learn ways to increase understanding these emotions and their expression. Within the social impairment (so called – I'd say again, different ability) of Asperger's Syndrome in terms of social relating does feeling or expressing empathy become more challenging or difficult for many with AS, yes. This has to do with the different ways that we process information. It has to do with the NT social context that most with AS, even when we understand it to varying degrees, do not find it to be the way that we engage, the way that we would relate that would be first-nature to us.

Many people with Asperger's Syndrome have a capacity for empathy; some more so than others, some maybe not so much. Again, Asperger's Syndrome is not the same for each and every person who has it. However, the blanket statement in the pathologizing DSM-IV definition of Asperger's Syndrome (which by the way is not even slated to exist as such in the upcoming DSM-V professionals now preferring it just be lumped in with autism so that everyone can get even more confused) that people with Asperger's lack empathy is not all that accurate. It is a statement without explanation; a statement, black-and-white as it is, that doesn't take into account each Aspie's individuality, and the reality that people can feel more than you can know. This is especially true when much that can be felt by those with Asperger's Syndrome isn't met with the same need for expression, socially or otherwise, often as it is for those who are neurotypical.

This begs the question how professionals can even really accurately assess what someone with Asperger's feels or has the capacity to feel. How can you know if I lack empathy just because perhaps I didn't express something that was wanted, coveted, expected or that NT's define as a "social norm"?

You really can't, can you?

Should we as people with Asperger's Syndrome, make up some book and pathologize NT's who have a greater need and/or desire to relate many things, empathy being perhaps one of those feelings, to others more often than we do because to us that is not "normal" or necessary?

I believe that most Aspies do feel empathy. I also believe that they want to experience empathy from others but that often both are lost in terms of expression and reception to the different ways in which we think, process information and to the different degrees to which we feel the need to actually "socialize".

That does not a lack of empathy make. That makes for difference. More difference that is not understood, not tolerated and that is pathologized by the "powers that be" who decide how it is that we are all "supposed" to relate to one another.

Small box that, don't you think?

Don't Freak Out

Chapter 10 Summary

- Words matter. Use them wisely.
- For better communication, remember the three S's: Specific, Simple and Safe.
- As Scott said in one of his poems, increased acceptance will lead to a brighter day.
- People with Asperger's can and do often find true love.
- People with Asperger's can be as empathetic and compassion as anyone else. They just may not express it in the same way.

Final Thoughts

Our autistic children grow up to be autistic adults. The kind of people they become is honestly their own choice. But as their parents, we have a responsibility to show them the different paths and make sure they have what they need to travel down them. How you choose to lead them is up to you.

Remember at the beginning when I said that if there was anything you got from reading this book, I hoped that it was that you find the strength to BELIEVE... in yourself, in your instincts and, above all, in your child! Do you believe?

Go back and reread the words that the six very different and diverse grownups with Asperger's wrote in last the chapter. Can you see your child in them? Do you hear his voice in your head while you read the words? If you don't yet, that's okay. Don't freak out. You are just not ready to hear them yet. But trust me on this, one day you will be. One day you will wake up and see that your child is just that... a child. The fact that he has Asperger's will no longer be anything more than a descriptive word, for it will just be part of what makes him the person he is – your unique, perfect, beautiful child. And that, my dear friends, is definitely nothing to Freak Out about!

Thanks for making it to the end of the book. You deserve a pat on the pack for that. Seriously, because I can tell you I don't usually make it to the end of self-help books. (Never enough bathroom time I guess. LOL)

Neil and I hope you will stay in contact. Please do not hesitate to shoot us a question. Below is our contact info, and we hope that you will take the time to reach out to us and let us know what you think about this book and, of course, how it is going with your child.

Book Website: www.aspieparenting.com

Sharon's email: sharon@sharonfuentes.com

Neil's email: neil@neilmcnerney.com

Sharon's interactive blog/facebook page :

www.facebook.com/MamasTurnNow

Neil's facebook page:

www.facebook.com/reducehomeworkstress

Our twitter names: @mamasturnnow and @neilmcnerney

Neil's parting advice is: Stay Calm and don't take it personally.

My parting advice to you is this: Remember to breathe and re-member that you are not alone! We are in this together, my friend. That is what being part of this club is all about!

   - Sharon and Neil

Acknowledgements

From Sharon:

It was never really my intention to write a book like this. Honestly, it just kind of happened. People would meet my boy and then me, and well, they would complement me on what a great job I was doing with him. Of course, I would graciously smile, but deep down I wanted to scream, "Um… you got it all wrong. I am not teaching him. He is teaching me!"

One day while walking with my dear friend Aivi, I came clean. I told her that everything I do is because of Jay. Who I am, the way I now think is because of him. She said to me, "Wow, you should write a book about that." I laughed, she laughed, and then we both stopped laughing because it suddenly seemed like a really good idea.

Of course, thinking about doing something and actually doing it are two completely different things. As my dear co-author Neil wrote in the back of his last book, "It either flowed like water or got stuck like granite." There are so many people I need to thank because without them this project would still have been stuck like granite.

I need to start with my sweet son Jay. One day while writing this book, I told him, "You know, you are my MUSE." He replied, "Great, then I want 12% of the books profit, one percent for every year I have been alive to inspire you!" How do you not get inspired and love a kid like that? Thank you for allowing me to share your stories with the world Jay. I am so proud to be your mother. Oh, and we'll discuss your 12% after you clean your room!

To my hubby, Roger, my cheerleader, my life coach my partner, thank you for encouraging me to go for it, whatever IT is at the time. For calming my fears, wiping my tears and giving me a good kick in the rear when I need it. I love you more than yesterday but less than tomorrow.

To my precious baby girl, Grace: Watching you grow into the incredible young woman you are becoming is truly a gift from above. Time after time you thoughtfully brought me a cup of coffee without me even asking or made your brother lunch so that I could keep writing when you saw the thoughts were flowing. Your unconditional love, support and contagious laugh always keep me going. I love you my Mini Me!

To my mother and father: No words can express how truly grateful I am for the amount of support you have always given me. Dad, for years you have told me that if you want something bad enough and are willing to work really hard for it; it can happen. Well it is happening dad! Now it's your turn!

To my mother in law, Maria: Yes I know I know… 10% for my agent. Seriously, thank you for supporting me and my dreams. I hope I make you proud!

To my sister, Arlene: You inspire me, as you are a living example of how you are never too old to go after your dreams. I promise to keep dreaming if you do sis!

To my brother, Dave: Well you certainly keep my ego in check now don't ya? Thanks for making sure my feet stay planted on the ground by never letting me forget that I am and always will be the BABY of the family! Seriously… you know you to are not too old for some dreaming, just saying!

To the rest of my family and all my wonderful friends and neighbors: You must all be glad this book is finally written because I am sure you are tired of me talking about it! I thank you all for commenting on my Facebook statuses and in person, for cheering and encouraging me on!

To Kate, Nicholas, Scott, Kansas, Charlie and A.J.: I thank you so much for sharing with me your words, your thoughts, emotions and selves. You inspire me to be a better person, a better mom and to definitely be a better question asker!

To all my fellow bloggers out there who were so kind to read and review this book: Thank you for your time, your thoughtful comments, support and for all your efforts you make every day in the name of Autism Acceptance.

To my online Mama's Turn Now Community: I have said it before and I will say it again here... we did it! We finished the book. You all have been there with me every step of the way and I am so grateful for that. Now go write a great review about this book on Amazon won't ya! LOL

To my editor, Jennifer: THANK YOU and yes it is in all capital letters and I may even throw in a run on sentence too. Editing this book was not an easy task but you took on the challenge and for that we are forever grateful to you. Thank you for offering us your professional and personal opinions and for making this book readable.

Lastly but certainly not least...to my co-author, Neil: Fellow author friends of mine have told me horror stories about their experiences co-authoring a book; but thankfully this project has been nothing but a joy. Neil you are not only knowledgeable, you are funny and have one of the biggest hearts around. I appreciate you taking me under your wing and showing me the ropes. Who would have thought that writing this thing was the easy part? Without you Neil... well there would be nothing without you. I am thankful to have had the opportunity to work with you, but even more so to be able to now call you my friend!

From Neil

I first met my co-author, Sharon Fuentes, during one of my parenting seminars at a local middle school. After the event, Sharon approached me and began the conversation by asking: "How would you like to write a book together?" I think I surprised myself as much as I surprised her by saying, "Sure! Let's start planning."

As I continue to grow in years, I have learned more and more to trust my first impression with people. I could tell that Sharon was someone that I could trust and work with. Fortunately, I was right. It has been a joy working with Sharon on this project, and I am excited to see what interesting opportunities this will provide us. Thanks, Sharon, for making this such an enjoyable process!

Thanks to my wife, Colleen, and my kids, Max and Shannon, for their support and encouragement during the writing process. Giving me the time to help create calm in families through my writing is a great gift to me and, hopefully, to many families.

An thanks to all the kids that I have worked with over the years that are on the spectrum and have struggled, strived, and thrived in their lives. Your insight and drive will always be an inspiration.

Resources

There is so much info on the web that it is difficult to sort through it all. The following pages will hopefully help you with this. The list is certainly not complete, but it will be a good starting point for you.

For a clickable online version of these resources, go to:

www.aspieparenting.com/resources

Abbreviations

You will find that people tend to throw around a bunch of letters and just assume you know what they mean. Below is a list of commonly used terms you may encounter.

- AAC - Augmentative and Alternative Communication
- ABA - Applied Behavior Analysis
- ADA - Americans with Disabilities Act
- ADD - Attention Deficit Disorder
- ADHD - Attention Deficit Hyperactivity Disorder
- AE - Age Equivalent
- AIT - Auditory Integration Therapy
- AS - Asperger's Syndrome
- ASD - Autistic Spectrum Disorder
- ASL - American Sign Language
- ASPIE -A person with Asperger's Syndrome
- BD/ED -Behavior Disordered / Emotionally Disturbed
- BOCES - Board of Cooperative Educational Services
- BOE - Board of Education
- BP - Bi-Polar
- CAPD - Central Auditory Processing Disorder
- CHAT - Checklist for Autism in Toddlers
- CNS - Central Nervous System
- CSE - Committee on Special Education

- DAS - Developmental Apraxia of Speech
- DD - Developmental Disability
- DSM - Diagnostic Statistical Manual
- DX - Diagnosis
- ED – Emotional Disability
- EEG – Electrocephalogram (used to test for seizures)
- EI - Early Intervention
- FAPE - Free and Appropriate Public Education
- FC - Facilitated Communication
- FERPA - Family Educational Rights and Privacy Act
- GARS - Gilliam Autism Rating Scale
- HFA - High Functioning Autism
- IDEA - Individuals with Disabilities Act
- IEP - Individualized Education Program
- IQ - Intelligence Quotient
- IFSP - Individualized Family Service Plan
- LD - Learning Disability (Learning Disabled)
- LRE - Least Restrictive Environment
- MRI -Magnetic Resonance Imaging
- NICHCY - National Information Center for Children and Youth with Disabilities
- NIH - National Institutes of Health
- NOS -Not Otherwise Specified, usually seen as PDD-NOS
- NT -Neurotypical
- OCD -Obsessive-Compulsive Disorder
- ODD -Oppositional-Defiant Disorder
- OHI - Other Health Impaired
- OT -Occupational Therapy
- PDD -Pervasive Developmental Disorder
- PT - Physical Therapy
- SED - State Education Department
- SEIT - Special Education Itinerant Teacher Services
- SETRC - Special Education Training Resource Centers
- SI - Sensory Integration
- SLP - Speech Language Pathologist
- SPD - Sensory Processing Disorder

- SPED - Special Education
- TEACCH -Treatment & Education of Autistic & Related Communication Disorders
- TOM -Theory of Mind
- TS -Tourette's Syndrome
- VESID - Office of Vocational & Educational Services for Individuals with Disabilities
- VI - Visually Impaired
- VR - Vocational Rehabilitation
- WISC -Wechsler Intelligence Scale for Children

National Autism and Asperger's Organizations

The information describing each resource comes directly from the organization itself. Most of these organizations have local chapters.

Autism Society of America

www.autismsociety.org

The leading voice and resource of the entire autism community in education, advocacy, services, research and support. Mission Statement: Improving the lives of all affected by autism.

Autism Speaks

www.autismspeaks.org

At Autism Speaks, our goal is to change the future for all who struggle with autism spectrum disorders. We are dedicated to funding global biomedical research into the causes, prevention, treatments and a possible cure for autism.

GRASP (Global and Regional Asperger Syndrome Partnership)

www.grasp.org

GRASP is an educational and advocacy organization for individuals with autism spectrum disorders offering information and autism resources.

OASIS (Online Asperger Syndrome Information and Support)

www.aspergersyndrome.org

Online Asperger Syndrome Information and Support (OASIS) center that joined with MAAP Services for Autism and Asperger Syndrome to create a single resource for families, individuals, and medical professionals who deal with the challenges of Asperger Syndrome, Autism, and Pervasive Developmental Disorder/ Not Otherwise Specified (PDD/NOS).

The National Autistic Society

www.autism.org.uk

The leading UK charity for people with autism (including Asperger syndrome) and their families. We provide information, support and pioneering services, and campaign for a better world for people with autism. This site also has a page that lists autism-related charities all around the world.

Educational Sources

IDEA

http://idea.ed.gov

The Individuals with Disabilities Education Act (IDEA) is a law put in place to ensure services to children with disabilities throughout the nation. IDEA governs how states and public agencies provide early intervention, special education and related services to more than 6.5 million eligible infants, toddlers, children and youth with disabilities.

Infants and toddlers with disabilities (birth-2) and their families receive early intervention services under IDEA Part C. Children and youth (ages 3-21) receive special education and related services under IDEA Part B. Visit the website at

Early Intervention Support

www.earlyinterventionsupport.com/resources/links/state.aspx

A great website that gives info on what Early Interventions are available state by state.

Do2learn

www.dotolearn.com

Do2learn provides thousands of free pages with social skills and behavioral regulation activities and guidance, learning songs and games, communication cards, academic material and transition guides for employment and life skills. My favorite section is the social skills toolbox. It's great stuff, and most of it is free!!!

I'm Determined

www.imdetermined.org

This website is filled with tools to help your child take control of his education and future. You will find templates for one-pagers, goal setting, and even a form to help the student figure out what he needs to do to have a good day at school.

Social Thinking

www.socialthinking.com

This site offers tons of articles and information as well as products to purchase such as games, books, DVDs etc. that can help our kids with perspective and other social skills that are sometimes hard for them.

Books

I highly suggest reading anything and everything by John Elder Robinson (*Raising Cubby, Be Different, Look Me in the Eye*), Tony Attwood (*Complete Guide to Asperger Syndrome* and others) and Temple Grandin (*The Way I See It, Thinking in Pictures, Animals in Translation*, and others).

Below are some lesser known books that the folks above even recommend .

Atypical: Life with Asperger's in 20 1/3 chapters - by Jesse Saperstein, a young Aspergian

Asperger's From the Inside Out - by GRASP founder Michael John Carley

Freaks, Geeks & Asperger Syndrome: A User Guide to Adolescence - by Luke Jackson

Of Mice and Aliens: An Asperger Adventure (Asperger Adventures) - by Kathy Hoopmann

Blue Bottle Mystery: An Asperger Adventure (Asperger Adventures) - by Kathy Hoopmann

Everybody Is Different: A Book for Young People Who Have Brothers or Sisters with Autism - by Fiona Bleach

Asperger's Huh? A Child's Perspective - by Rosina G. Schnurr and John Strachan

Songs of the Gorilla Nation - by Dawn Prince Hughes

The Sensory Sensitive Child - by Karen A. Smith and Karen R. Gouze

Alone Together - by Katrin Bentley

Making Peace with Autism - by Susan Senator

All I Can Handle - by Kim Stagliano.

Mom and Dad Support Pages and Blogs

There are tons of online Autism/Asperger's support blogs, Facebook pages and communities. Along the way I have come across quite a few wonderful folks, some of whom I am now honored to call my friends. There are way too many to include them all, so I am just going to give you a few diverse ones and encourage you to search out more. A good collection of both parent blogs and blogs written by folks with Asperger's can be found at the Autism Blog Directory - autismblogsdirectory.blogspot.com.

Of course I would love for you to join me and my community over at Mama's Turn Now on Facebook as well.

A Chameleon in the Spectrum

www.chameleoninthespectrum.wordpress.com

This page is a place where you can share your challenges and rewards of parenting in the Autism Spectrum and parenting in general.

Adventures in Asperger's

www.adventuresinaspergers.com

A blog by a father of 3,one with Asperger's and another with Anxiety Disorder, they get by with humor and chicken nuggets.

Adventures in Extreme Parenting

www.extremeparenthood.com

Sunday is one frazzled mom raising two boys with autism while living to laugh and blog about it.

Confessions of an Asperger's Mom

www.confessionsofanaspergersmom.blogspot.com
www.facebook.com/groups/AspergersConfessions
This Autism/Asperger's community support page is a place to share information, celebrate victories, vent, whine, wine, cry and most of all laugh with others who are on the same journey. If you have a teen with Asperger's, you need to read Karen's blog.

Diary of a Mom

www.adiaryofamom.wordpress.com

Jess says, "It is a sense of community that makes the good times sweeter for the sharing and the hard times more bearable for knowing that we're not alone." Here you will find some of the most sincere and beautiful writing I have ever seen.

Living on the Spectrum: The Conner Chronicles

theconnorchronicles.wordpress.com

Flannery blogs about whatever random amusement comes to her mind but mostly about her son Conner who has severe ADHS and mild Asperger's.

Stimeyland

www.stimeyland.com

Stimey believes that rodents are funny, autism may be different than you think and that if you have a choice between laughing and crying, you should always try to laugh—although sometimes you may have to do both.

The Real Housewives of Autism Facebook Page

www.facebook.com/therealhousewivesofautism

This page is run by some of your favorite autism mom bloggers. They are rude, crude and let's just say if you are easily offended, it is not a place for you. But if you enjoy a bit of snarky fun, then head on over to their party.

Yeah, Good Times

www.yeahgoodtimes.blogspot.com

Snarky, Mama to 2 boys: Child 1 is autistic and Child 2 OMG isn't. She writes about...stuff. Sometimes. Other times she writes about other stuff. A lot of the time she doesn't write anything at all. She is hysterical but as a warning...not G-rated!

Folks w/Asperger's Support Blogs and Pages

ThAutcast: Asperger's and Autism Community

www.theautcast.com

thAutcast brings together news and entertainment for people with autism and Asperger's and people who are interested in us.

Wrong Planet

www.wrongplanet.net

This is the web community designed for individuals (and parents/professionals of those) with Autism, Asperger's Syndrome, ADHD, PDDs and other neurological differences. They provide a discussion forum where members communicate with each other, an article section with exclusive articles and how-to guides, a blogging feature and a chat room for real-time communication with other Aspies.

Online Games Made for Our Kids

AutCraft

www.autcraft.com

This is the first Minecraft server dedicated to providing a safe and fun learning environment for children on the autism spectrum and their families. (It is free, but you must have a Minecraft account.)

Whiz Kid Games

www.whizkidgames.com

This is a site for young kids with autism. Games focus on such things as matching emotions, dealing with change, social interactions and more. Graphics are basic, but young kids will find them fun, colorful and enjoyable.

Play Time with Zeebu

www.playtimewithzeebu.com

The free online games found here deal with recognizing emotions, calming techniques and memory skills. Zeebu the monkey is cute, but I have to admit that the music in the background, while soothing to kids, can really get on a parent's nerves. Whip out those headphones and let your youngster explore the world of Zeebu.

Tools and Products

The items below are ones that seem to be helpful for kids with Asperger's. Check out www.aspieparenting.com/resources

Visual Timer- We use one of these with Jay. It helps with transitions as it is a visual cue. For kids who have a hard time with the abstract concept of time, this helps immensly.

Indoor Trampoline- It is ideal for children who crave vestibular motion and is a great way to develop gross motor skills and balance. Not to mention, it's good exercise too!

Noise-reducing Headphones- Children with auditory processing issues find many noises highly disturbing and the use of sound-reducing headphones provides temporary relief is and can help turn unpleasant situations into more bearable ones.

Fidgets- These are a great way to keep restless fingers busy, bodies relaxed and minds focused! Fidgets can be a very helpful self-regulation tool at homework time, in waiting rooms, restaurants, in the car, while riding the school bus, and more.

Weighted Blanket- Weighted blankets offer a slight hug and therefore have shown to generate proprioceptive input on our bodies. For many, this causes the brain to release neurotransmitters like serotonin and dopamine that have calming effects which usually translate to a better night's sleep.

36011283R00102

Made in the USA
Lexington, KY
03 October 2014